ARE YOU
OVER
PARENTING?

Lachmi Deb Roy, a special correspondent with *Outlook* magazine, has been a lifestyle journalist for the past fifteen years. She has worked with, and written for, leading publications such as *The Hindu*, *The Times of India* and lifestyle magazines. In 2013, she was the cultural ambassador to Mexico on behalf of Rotary International. As a lifestyle journalist, she likes to work on sensitive and research-based stories on children and women's issues. The mother of a thirteen-year-old, Lachmi lives with her husband in Delhi. A sepsis survivor and an autoimmune warrior, she believes in living each day of her life to the fullest.

ARE YOU OVER PARENTING?

WHY DOING EVERYTHING POSSIBLE HARMS YOUR CHILD

Lachmi Deb Roy

RUPA

Published by
Rupa Publications India Pvt. Ltd 2019
7/16, Ansari Road, Daryaganj
New Delhi 110002

Sales Centres:
Allahabad Bengaluru Chennai
Hyderabad Jaipur Kathmandu
Kolkata Mumbai

ISBN: 978-81-291-515-1

First impression 2019

10 9 8 7 6 5 4 3 2 1

The moral right of the author has been asserted.

Printed at HT Media Ltd, Gr. Noida

Disclaimer

This work is based on my experience as a mother and also on conversations with many parents. I have used certain sections from my previously published articles in *The Times of India* and *The Hindu*, and permissions have been taken from both. Names of some people have been changed on request to protect their identities. The reader should exercise his or her judgement in using the tips suggested in this book, as I am not a qualified expert or physician. I hope this book helps you on your journey of parenting.

Contents

Introduction

Most of us parents today walk a tightrope between raising children and managing careers. If we miss work, we think that overtime will make up for it. But if we miss our child's (Parent-teacher Meeting) PTM or annual concert, then overtime never really helps, and the subsequent guilt lasts forever. This makes me wonder: are we not pushing on the parental pedal too hard? When I say 'we', I refer to a new breed of hyper parents who want to have it all.

Who are these new-age parents? you may ask. The new-age parents expect the best: be it the child's behaviour or performance. This is because society expects them to excel. This forces parents to emphasize more on short-term goals than long-term goals which improve the confidence of a child. We forget that excessive involvement in our child's life can impede their emotional and mental growth.

Can we admit that at some point of time we are overdoing our job as parents? Although well-intended, we don't realize when to stop the urge to parent. We all want the best for our children, but it is time for parents to sit back and realize the importance of letting go.

In this book, I share my experiences of being the mother of a thirteen-year-old, and try to explain how I resisted the impulse of being a hyper parent, in the hope that it will help you too. My advice, which is just a suggestion, is to make your child's growing-up years simple and uncomplicated.

As a lifestyle journalist for the last fifteen years, I have written mostly on health, food and social issues for leading English dailies like *The Times of India* and *The Hindu*. Presently, I am working with *Outlook* magazine as a special correspondent. I have written on parenting extensively for all the publications that I have worked for, even before becoming a mother. My colleagues used to make fun of me and say that motherhood would be a cakewalk for me. I have always considered parenting to be my primary job. This book holds a very special place in my heart since parenting is a topic that I can relate to, even with my eyes closed.

There is another reason why the topic is close to my heart. When my husband, who is in the Indian Navy, was transferred to Russia, my son was just forty-one days old. I was a new parent, that too in an alien country, and with bitter climate to beat. Managing everything on my own and single parenting most of the time, I have learnt parenting the hard way. The bond that I have now developed with my son is something that I am proud of. I realized during my stay in Russia, when I was single-handedly managing my newborn and adjusting to the climate, that anything you give your heart and soul to, be it parenting or your job, you are bound to be happy with the outcome.

From a full-time lifestyle journalist, I became the master cleaner of poop and puke. There were days when being a mother used to give me euphoric highs, followed by days of sinking lows. The day my son was born, I knew I was going to be a slave to this cherubic, bubble-blowing pink ball. Those were the days when he used to influence every decision of my life and I don't think much has changed even today. Freedom, self-indulgence and career took a backseat and I became an expert in baby babble. I won't say that I am not enjoying motherhood, but it has its own ups and downs, and one should be prepared for them before taking the plunge.

Those initial days, when we shifted to Russia as new parents, were the toughest days of our married life. There were days when I used to sink into depression, but motherhood made me stronger and smarter. For instance, I learnt how to breastfeed my baby while cooking. There were days when I overfed my child, but I learnt from my mistakes. And the best thing about single parenting is that I know my child inside out.

Like all other parents I also suffered from the same pressures and fears. I spoke to many parents and also to child psychologists and teachers to get their views on parenting. I would love to hear from parents of special children, as I have dedicated a chapter to special children, a topic which needs to be handled with a lot of sensitivity and care.

If you have read my writings on parenting in leading publications, you will find the style similar in this book. Like a journalist, and, most importantly, being a mother who is a journalist, I like to justify my writing with quotes from experts.

I feel every stage of parenting has its own share of highs and lows, and there are actually no theories for bringing up children. We live in an age of hyperinformation which is the main cause of our confusion and we end up hyper-parenting. This book is for every new-age parent. It looks at how over-involvement can harm the child in the long run. I am no expert, but I realized that my experiences as a mother and also as a professor of media studies helped me understand young minds. My younger colleagues ask for suggestions on a lot of things, especially their careers and their personal life.

In the last chapter, I also talk about how parents should take care of themselves. I learnt this the hard way when I was diagnosed with a life-threatening disease called sepsis. The doctors said that my body had been sending signals, but I had probably not paid attention to it because I was so busy carrying out my duties in the best possible way. Being an urban working mother, whose husband is not around during most of the growing-up years of the child, is not an easy task. I learnt a lesson that I need to be fit first, to be able to take care of my child.

To all the parents out there, I want to convey that while

parents' love for their children is undeniable, we, as parents, should not be overambitious. Wanting them to do well is not wrong, but remember that your child is not your possession! If you nag about every small thing, and want everything for them and by them to be done to perfection, then that is a sign of hyper-parenting. So, let's solve the riddle of parenting together!

1

Trials of Being a Gen Next Parent

Many parents today feel that being a parent is like having a full-time job. They have been programmed to believe that the ticket to their child's success is in their hands. In fact, the preparation to bring up the perfect child starts even before they are born. Parents are turning their children into mini robots and schedule slaves.

I believe that overparenting reflects in the parent's desire to manage every single decision of their child, not giving them the scope to decide what they like or dislike.

As parents, we all have our highs and lows, times when we are proud of our parenting, as well as times when we are totally embarrassed about the way we have brought up our children.

There was a time when I used to make my son participate in each and every competition that took place in school, starting from fancy dress to painting and elocution, even academics-based activities like Math-O-Fun and Spell-O-Fun. Although my son was always interested in sports, we wanted him to paint and also play the piano. We never realized that there is no fun in competitions if a child is pushed to participate in every single thing. I didn't even bother to ask if he was happy doing these things. I thought he was too young and I wanted him to be an all-rounder in everything. Today I regret the fact that I had pushed him too hard to do things which he didn't really enjoy.

When he told us one day that piano was something *we* wanted him to play and that he liked playing games and sports in his free time, it was a total eye-opener for us.

I asked myself if I had actually been ruling his life. Was I getting into a power struggle for every little thing? Am I one of those parents who struggle to allow the child to make his own choices? Am I one of those parents who jump to the rescue of my child whenever I get the faintest feeling that he is failing? Am I overburdening my child with my own failed dreams? I sat down peacefully and asked myself these questions again and again. The answers to all these questions were a loud and clear 'YES'. The bottom line is: I was overparenting. I was stunting the growth of my child by overprotecting and overindulging him.

This does not mean that I should not care or worry about him. I am still petrified by the fact that my child has to cross the road on his own. So, am I overcaring or overparenting? It is easy to say that we are a bunch of caring parents who dedicate all their time to their children, but actually we are suffocating them with excess love and care.

Parenting is not a race

Often I see that we see and treat our children as competitors, always running a race with an undefined finishing line. And with each passing year, the expectations of the so-called new-age parents are increasing. We are always discussing our children among ourselves or thinking of ways to keep them engaged. When my husband takes my son for a game of golf, he says that is his free time. Here again, we are trying to mould his life to meet *our* expectations.

A child's free time should be completely unorganized. We don't want them to waste a single minute. We want them to make the best use of their time. If a group of parents are having a chat outside school or a hobby class, they are only discussing ways to give the best to their child, and in the process, they end up pressurizing the child. We rarely seem to be happy with the achievements of our children. We want them to excel in everything. Are we really happy if our child gets an eight out of ten or do we want, or rather demand, a ten out of ten from them in each and every activity?

We are forgetting that parenting is not a race we need to win. Over-burdening and excessive criticism from us can take a mental toll on the child. Paediatricians say children as young as five are suffering from anxiety attacks. If your child is over-burdened, they will most likely be overtly clingy, bite their nails, throw tantrums, suck their thumbs and sometimes pull out their hair and wet their beds. The cause of all this is the new parenting trend that pushes parents to unlock their child's potential early in life; otherwise, they feel that their children will not grow up to be successful adults. Parenting, indeed, has become a very competitive thing. It is time parents start taking things a little easy by accepting their child's shortcomings and, at the same time, being happy with the unique qualities that the child possesses.

Parents need to focus on the emotional development of the child, instead of focusing only on intellectual development. And as parents we should remember that we play a crucial role in fostering healthy emotional development in children. In fact, it is the parents' behaviour that plays a crucial role in how a child develops into an emotionally secure adult. Friends start playing a very important role during teenage. It is up to us to give them exposure to a good circle of friends who will have a positive influence in their lives.

We should be more aware of our moods; only then can we take care of our child's emotional requirements effectively. The other day, I had pressed the panic button a bit too hard. I was definitely stressed out with my own work, but at the same time, I was stressed out that my son's eighth standard, yes eighth standard, final exams were approaching. My husband and I continued pestering him that he should reduce his playtime and finish the syllabus. 'Did you finish your Social Science syllabus? How on earth are you going to get an A1 in it?' I guess we all do this because we live in a world of cutthroat competition. We should blame ourselves, not the education system, because we forcibly made ourselves slaves to the system, and we expect our children to do the same. Our parents didn't score 98 per cent and 99 per cent marks in board exams, and they are not fools. I am sure most of us also didn't score that kind of marks in exams. Then is it fair for us to ask our children to score such high percentages? Should we mimic and follow a vicious cycle blindly?

Do you want a perfect child?

Children are automatically burdened by undue responsibilities of scoring that 90-something per cent. In real work life, which all children have to step into one day, will your school marks actually have much of a role to play? As a parent, ask yourself: Do you have a lot of expectations from your child? If so, you are likely to damage their emotional growth.

It is not exams that parents want their child to excel

in. Seema Hingorrany, a psychologist, friend and author of *Beating the Blues,* a book on depression, told me about a parent who brought her child, suffering from severe depression, to see her. 'After speaking to the girl for a long time, I got to know that this started with her mother wanting her to look like her cousin sister. It became a kind of competition for the mother.'

The time we used to spend in making sandcastles or playing with Barbie dolls, has given way to piano lessons, football practice, maths tuitions, science tuitions…and the list is endless. We now judge our children on every aspect of their performance in class, be it sports or academics. Raising the next Tiger Woods or Serena Williams has become more important for parents than raising a happy and emotionally stable child. Resist the pressure of expecting children to excel in whatever they do. Such pressures have adverse effects by burning them out too early in life. If we pressurize our children too much, with academics and extracurricular activities, a time might come when they will lose interest in everything. For example, if we make our fourth-standard children solve number problems from the eighth standard, and expect them to stay ahead of their peers, when the right time comes and they actually need to dedicate more time to studies, they will not be able to do so because they will be totally exhausted by then.

Cost of expectations

New-age parents are letting guilt come in the way of enjoying the true purpose of parenting. This is primarily because of the decline of the joint family system. There was a time when there were many people in a family to take care of our children. Now, it is just the parents going through the ups and downs of parenthood, and they are not having it easy.

Parenting has also gone through a tremendous change with the times. Parents gear themselves up years before becoming parents. Apart from attending workshops, there are hundreds of books on the subject. In fact, workshops have become classrooms for parenting.

It is a challenging task, especially when both parents are working. Parents are likely to obsess over their children because of the guilt that they have not given enough time to them. In fact, I have often bribed my child with chocolates and toys to make up for time spent away from him.

Then, there are full-time parents who force their dreams on their children, sometimes unknowingly burdening them with undue parental pressures at a young age when they are supposed to play and have a good time.

I wonder if parents feel like failures because their child did not perform up to their expectations.

The first time I realized I had taken the wrong route to parenting was during my son's Civics exams. I generally spend time with him during revision by making him write all the answers and making him read all the chapters from the text book, and then testing him orally from the chapters. My husband warned me a number of times, that by spoon-feeding him, I was killing the individuality of the child. I realized, that's exactly what had happened. There was just one chapter which I had not revised with him and a question was asked from that chapter. Although he said he had finished revising, he had actually not revised properly before the exam. Unlike most chapters, I had not sat down with him on the day before the exam with that chapter. I later realized spoon-feeding had made him irresponsible. So, when a question came from that chapter, he was unable to answer it. The first step towards sensible parenting is accepting your mistake. We are humans and it is human to err, but the next step is about rectifying the mistake.

It is commonly seen that women these days are delaying pregnancy, as they choose to give time to their careers. Some choose to quit their jobs for parenting. The latter is when the parent is likely to see parenting as a full-time job.

Although it is reasonable as parents to want your child to be successful, this doesn't call for thrusting your dreams on them. It is important that the parents sit and have a heart to heart with their children. We need to have realistic expectations from them. Of course, that does not mean we keep the expectations so low that the children do not realize what they are capable of achieving.

By over-pressurizing the child, we are killing their individuality. Every child is unique. They are different individuals and we should never make the mistake of comparing them either with their siblings or with their friends. We are not here to programme them. Our duty is to guide them in the right direction.

There is a difference between suggesting and ordering. When you ask your child to do something, for instance, try to keep the tone mild. Keep their wants and interests in mind. When we bring children into the world, we give them a checklist of what we think success, failure, beauty and achievement are all about. But do we give them the ability to develop themselves and their abilities? It is time we parents realize that children are okay and whole as they are.

2

Are You Overparenting?

From the beginning, parents drill a competitive spirit and the need to be number one into the hearts and minds of the young. The need is to allow the child to be away from structured activities for some hours in a day. Let them play by themselves or just sit and dream with their eyes open. Whatever they want to do, we must let them feel good in their ordinariness.

Overparenting can not only stop your child from enjoying their childhood but also from growing up to be a responsible adult. I was quite taken aback when my son asked me if there had ever been a time when I had actually talked to him. He was right; that apart from telling him to eat and study, I rarely talked to him as an adult or at least as a teenager preparing to be one. I wondered how many times we talked about things that really matter, not just achievements and marks, but life in general, or nature. I must say, the answer is, very rarely.

We can always blame the upcoming event, such as the mid-semester exams, end-semester exams, final exams, piano lessons and school projects. The list is actually endless. But do we realize we will never get this time back? Hold on to those long goodnight kisses, those dining table chats, the walk in the park. When we don't get time for any of these, I feel we are truly overparenting. The dining table conversations I used to have as a child with my parents, are a thing of the past. It is the same for the long evening walks and stargazing. We may have become so busy in bringing up our children and trying to equip them with the ability to make a living that we have forgotten to give them the simple pleasures of life. As children, we used to go for walks on cold winter evenings to buy corns on the cob, roasted and then rubbed with lemon, chilli and black salt. When I took my son for the same, he said, 'Mama, don't you think having roadside stuff is unhygienic? You only talk about infections and tummy upsets.' I had no answer at that time, but I realized that our children are missing out on a lot of fun that we had as children.

Summer vacations for me were a season for plucking mangoes, both the green and the ripe yellow ones, eating them without washing my hands or the mangoes. We didn't even bother to cut them. All we had to do was bite into the skin and pull it off to reach the flesh, the juice dripping all over our arms. Those were the simple pleasures of life which our children have not enjoyed. Now they see the genetically modified and artificially sweetened fruits and they want them to be cut to perfection and served with a fork. When I narrate these stories to my son, he asks me (and this is quite distressing) whether the mangoes those days looked ugly or were as spotless and 'perfect' as those in the market that he sees.

I know then that it is necessary for him to try and love the perfectly imperfect things that life has to offer, because that is where true beauty lies.

Prominent signs of overparenting

If you find yourself nodding to the following statements under the broad categories, then it is likely that you have been overparenting.

Being authoritative

- ✘ You are strict about little things like eating every morsel of food on the plate.
- ✘ You argue with your five-year-old about keeping the bed clean.
- ✘ You end up constantly telling your thirteen-year-old what to wear for which occasion, what sports they should be playing and which friends they should be talking to in class.

If you agreed to some or all of these statements, then it's time to give your child a break. Remember that we are here to guide our children and not to rule over their lives. Children have a mind of their own. In fact, many a time we don't allow our children to make their own choices. Don't think about whether they are right or wrong, because there is no such thing. Just let the child do things their way and that is going to be the best way for you to support them, as parents.

Fearing failure

- ✗ You are scared of your child failing.
- ✗ You just can't stand the idea of your child not doing well, even in their first-standard exam.
- ✗ You are scared of your child not reciting their rhymes well, not presenting their project well in front of their class.

If you have agreed to these statements, then it is likely that you jump to your child's rescue at the slightest hint of a problem, complete their homework for them, make them learn by rote—like a parrot—and expect them to do things just the way you want them to.

Being overprotective

- ✗ You end up having a fight with others because they are ill-treating your child.
- ✗ You complain about the class teacher for not giving enough attention to your child.
- ✗ You argue when your child is not placed in the first row of a group dance performance on stage.

If you find yourself constantly arguing with coaches, teachers, caregivers and even grandparents and relatives about your child, then you are surely overparenting. Another thing I have seen is that parents do everything for their child, such as getting them a glass of water or feeding them. Many a time, we don't give our children any responsibilities, and we keep pampering and overindulging them. Remember, we need to assign chores to our children if we want them to be independent. Once the child gets into the habit of being dependent on their parents, it becomes very difficult for them to come out of their shell and do things on their own. If we don't assign some jobs to children, they will never be able to learn any life skills. One of my friends once narrated how difficult it was for her daughter to adjust to hostel life when she left home for college. She had not been used to doing any chores at home, and, at the same time, she always had her parents hovering around her, making her finish her homework, teaching her each and every subject, helping her overcome every hurdle in life. Basically, she became too dependent on her parents.

If your child is in college, then overparenting can lead to anxiety and a decline in the ability to cope with problems of everyday life, so it is best not to treat them like babies who need your guidance and attention more often. Such children are always bogged down by their parents' expectations and fear of how people are going to judge them. Diffidence in a child can be caused by an overprotective, over-controlling style of parenting. It may prevent young people from learning how to solve their problems and take responsibility for their lives.

Generally speaking, children born in the seventies and early eighties, who I presume are now mothers of pre-teens, teenagers and even college-goers, were raised with the freedom to play outside until sunset. And we all played unstructured games—running around in fields and gardens, playing hide-and-go-seek, and we came back home all sweaty and muddy, took a shower and sat down for a hearty meal with our parents. It was such a beautiful ritual, discussing how we spent the whole day and eating a home-cooked meal.

More than thirty years later, we live in an age where children play inside the house with their latest gadgets. If they want to play outside, it is structured games like golf and tennis. But, it is not they who have chosen it—we have introduced them to this habit. I remember, as children, if we were playing outside, we used to drink tap water. But it is we who have introduced our children to filtered and bottled water. It is we who have taught them to use hand sanitizers and wet wipes to stay away from germs.

We are responsible for this and I would be lying if I said that I don't do it myself. We don't want our children to feel the heat, so we travel in air-conditioned cars. We don't want them to sweat in the house, so we switch on the AC indoors too. We don't want them to get dirty and tanned by playing in the field, so we tell them to stay at home and introduce them to gadgets. We decide for them what outdoor sports to play. How are they to blame? I have heard parents say that they want the best for their children, and in this desire for finding the best for them, they hover over them and literally cover them in bubble wrap all the time. At the same time, we don't want our children to fail at anything in life. We want the best for them. The best is to follow the middle path. Don't be overprotective and, at the same time, don't be overtly lenient.

We need to ask ourselves first: are we overparenting? And if yes, we have taken the hardest step of being self-aware.

3

Every Child Is Unique

We all remember and cherish the first epic moments of our child—be it the first smile, the first step, the first turning around or the first fall. Surely, they are beautiful memories, but you will be surprised to learn that according to paediatricians, they are all developmental milestones and key skills that give an insight into your little one's development. The first milestone is the most important thing that parents wait for, because I have seen many parents panicking if the child has not covered each milestone on time. One of my friends was worried that her son didn't have his first tooth till the time he was six months old, when infants generally have it by four months. So, when she went to the doctor with her worry, he said, 'Have you ever seen a grown-up without teeth? So, just give him time and understand that some things take time for some children.'

As a young parent, keep in mind that every child is unique in their own way. We generally tend to get competitive and start comparing our child with the neighbour's children, or go by the book. Comparing our child with anybody else's is the biggest mistake we can commit. If every child is different, why should they be compared with another? Developmental milestones like turning over, sitting without back support, lifting up the head, crawling, walking and talking always don't occur in a predictable way.

It is natural for the child to learn to crawl and walk on their own. If the child doesn't fall, they are never going to learn. A child, while learning to walk, falls at least 38 to 40 times a day and it is perfectly okay. Avoid jumping to their rescue every time they fall. Let them fall and learn to get up on their own. Babies are built to fall and get up on their own. They are built in such a way that they all learn to walk, talk and run on their own. Just give them time. Some children take a little longer, while others do them pretty early. But that does not mean they are not good enough! I have seen many parents labelling their children as 'fast' or 'slow'. The biggest thing that you can do for your child is to accept them for who they are and stop comparing and labelling them. If you have not done this so far, it is not too late even now. Make a conscious effort to do so now.

As your child steps into toddlerhood from infancy, allow them to make mistakes. For instance, give them a small mid-morning snack and allow them to eat it on their own. Bear with the mess and remember—all children learn to eat by being messy initially. When my son was barely eight or nine months old, I used to give him finger food, and he used to happily eat on his own, though he used to hate the mashed potatoes and other baby food. In this way, he learnt to eat by himself very early in life. Sometimes a child takes exceptionally long to reach a milestone, and then you might consider taking them to the doctor. But, in general, avoid panicking and blaming yourself if these milestones don't happen on time because babies are not like pre-packaged food that they will be cooked right on time.

Nature versus nurture

Do parents have any effect on the long-term development of children? Some believe that everything is predestined, but others believe that parents' behaviour has a huge influence on children. The nature versus nurture debate may be age-old, but the fact remains that each child is different, hence they face different challenges at different points in life. As parents, we should ensure that we provide the right environment for the overall development of the child, which includes mental health and well-being. The family plays an important role in creating a real environment to nurture the young mind, and this can happen only if we consciously spend time in the lap of nature.

Peers too influence children, especially in the teenage years. Yet parents can have a much greater influence on the personality traits and value system of our children. The choices that you may make as a parent have a tremendous effect on the choices the children make when they grow up.

For instance, parents need to ask themselves whether they are practising what they are preaching. If you ask your child to switch off, you must consciously practise it.

Parents need to use their influence carefully, especially when children are in the pre-teen and early teen age group.

One of the biggest responsibilities that parents need to fulfil is to inculcate good habits in their children. They should know not to interrupt when two adults are talking, and to talk to everybody politely and respectfully. Of course, it is a task easier said than done, but these good habits are the foundation of the child's personality.

Remember that the road of parenting is full of stumbling blocks for all parents and that one must find a way around them.

4

Teach Your Child Life Skills

'It is not what you do for your children, but what you have taught them to do for themselves, that will make them successful human beings.'

—Ann Landers
American advice columnist

If you are a parent who nodded to most of the points in the (last section of the) previous chapter, then you will also agree that you tend to focus more on academic score development and not on life skills. What are life skills? The

World Health Organization (WHO) defines life skills as the abilities for adaptive and positive behaviour that enable individuals to deal effectively with demands and challenges of everyday life.

These are essential tools which parents need to consciously imbibe in their children from the early years, for them to face life more confidently as they grow up to be independent.

Even in the ancient scriptures like the Bhagavad Gita or the Puranas, life skills have been an important aspect for effective survival among human beings. Spiritual leaders and books talk about the importance of values through the help of stories which give real-life examples.

Life skills may sound simple, but the fact remains that one needs to put in a great deal of thought, time and effort to develop these skills in adulthood. Therefore, if children are taught these at a young age, it becomes easy to master them and incorporate them in their lives.

When there is so much negativity around us, it is important to introduce children to spiritual reading, teaching them the art of loving and forgiving. One doesn't need to go to a class to learn life skills. They can be taught at home and by you, the parents.

These skills prepare children for challenges in life, making them emotionally stronger, helping them cope with difficult situations and understand how to take decisions in life in the long term. By overparenting and over-protecting your child, you are not preparing them for life.

It is important that as parents we teach the following skills so that children can sail through the ups and downs of life.

Important life skills[1]

1. Problem-solving

Children face many challenges as they grow up, whether it is while starting school, joining a sports team or selecting peer groups. No matter how experienced you are as a parent, there are times when you end up making mistakes. I attended a workshop conducted by my friend, Payal

---

[1]Lachmi Deb Roy, 'The Winning Skills', *Mumbai Mirror*, 5 May 2018, https://mumbaimirror.indiatimes.com/others/health-lifestyle/the-winning-skills/articleshow/64036733.cms[© Bennett, Coleman & Co. Ltd.]

Shah, a child counsellor. She said that the ability to take decisions and solve problems on their own helps children cope with challenges in life in the long run. Children need to be taught how to identify problems, generate ideas for solutions and learn to try to solve problems on their own. Parents shouldn't run to their rescue all the time; instead, they should allow them to go wrong. They should give them a few chances to figure things out for themselves. Talking about her technique, Shah said, 'I divide the children into groups and give them situations, and they are asked to come out with solutions through roleplays. This helps them to work as a team, and at the same time, they learn to tackle problems independently.'

2. Decision-making

Whenever I have a doubt regarding parenting, I turn to my child counsellor and friend, psychotherapist Padma Rewari, who says that giving children opportunities to take decisions in their day-to-day lives develops a sense of responsibility in them. When they are allowed to make choices, they feel important and are careful about themselves. We, as parents, should allow children to identify the decisions to be taken and think and evaluate the options. We should encourage children to pen down their thoughts and feelings and talk to them about real-life situations and ask them what their decisions would be in such cases.

Most children are comfortable with what is known as programmed decisions. These are decisions for which there are clear rules and guidelines. The real test comes in unprogrammed decisions, for which they rely purely on their own judgement.

When in a crisis, most adults tend to take emotional decisions that they regret later. Even young children choose how they will behave, which games they would like to play, which books they would like to read and which television shows they would like to watch. As they get older, children take bigger decisions. The kind of decisions children make can affect their well-being. The Bhagavad Gita talks of the path of sreyas (good) versus the path of preyas (pleasant). Children should be taught to choose the path of sreyas and not take impulsive decisions. The path of preyas, on the other hand, forces you to take decisions that lead to instant gratification, which is not ideal in the long run.

3. Independence

'Independent thinking skills are very important for a child's development,' Dr Zirak Marker, child and adolescent psychiatrist, tells me. He adds, 'Children should be taught the importance of being different, and not just try to live up to everyone's expectations. This will help them be more accepting of themselves and build their own unique identities.' He talks about giving them the liberty to think for themselves and says that by unknowingly doing all the work for them, we can actually hinder the child's independent thinking skills. 'Independent thinking will help in boosting their self-esteem and confidence level.'

4. Creativity

Shah says in her workshop that children who are encouraged to think creatively exhibit higher self-esteem and motivation. Creative experiences can help children express their feelings and cope with them in a better way. In order to do this, they need to have an open mind and not be bogged down by restrictive thinking. To stand out in a crowded and competitive world and bring about change, children need to be able to think differently. Parents must inculcate the faculty of imagination in children. Brainstorming sessions and puzzles help children think creatively.

Dr Marker feels that creative thinking helps the child to think out of the box, and encourages them to follow their passion. We should encourage them to ask more questions and create their own art. Schools may not allow creativity to flourish, so you can take charge and allow them to get playful with colours. True art is all about enjoying and being in the moment.

5. Critical thinking

Ellen Galinsky, the author of *Mind in the Making,* talks about critical thinking in her list of seven essential life skills needed by every child. Critical thinking helps in mental growth. Children should be able to critically analyse information and differentiate between right and wrong. Parents should ask open-ended questions to awaken their thinking process. Ask questions as to why you think something is happening and what is causing that thing to happen. This, in the long run, helps in building analytical skills. Shah says that developing a holistic vision, with different ways of looking at a piece of information, as mentioned in the Bhagavad Gita, can be used for critical thinking.

6. Self-awareness

Children who are self-aware are better able to recognize their skills. Shah says, 'Self-awareness is a skill that helps children tune in to their feelings, thoughts and actions. This means children are able to keep track of what they are doing and figure out what's working and what's not working for them.' She adds that one of the reasons behind suicides in young adults is a lack of self-awareness. Shah says, 'Self-awareness also leads to self-reflection—thinking over things that happened, in order to find ways to make things work better next time. If children are aware of their strengths and weaknesses, it helps them make better decisions, understand and talk about their feelings and see how their behaviour affects others.' Ask your child to maintain a diary and pen down their thoughts, ideas, feelings and behaviour patterns to understand themselves.

7. Building interpersonal relationships

The happiness and satisfaction of every individual depend on what their interpersonal relationships are like. We live in a society that has an ever-increasing number of nuclear families, divorces, suicides and insensitivity towards others. Helping children develop the full range of interpersonal skills is one of the most important things we can do to ensure they grow up to have healthy relationships with others. Developing good interpersonal relationships help children become flexible adults. Developing the attitude of gratitude in children helps them value relationships, says Shah.

Dr Marker stresses on teaching the child to maintain good relationships with others. 'It is very important to work as a team, as there are very few jobs that don't require teamwork.'

8. Empathy

Shah's workshops encourage roleplays and discussions on empathy by teaching children to be good to others. She says, 'Empathy is seeing with the eyes of another, listening with the ears of another, and feeling with the heart of another. Children must be able to put themselves in other people's shoes to understand what they are feeling. They need to learn to get rid of all biases and prejudices, and think from others' points of view.'

Dr Marker says, 'As parents, we should encourage our children to understand the feelings of others. It is important that we provide constant emotional support to our children. Our children are going to learn from us how we treat the elderly and domestic helps in our house. This helps them feel for those in pain.'

9. Money management

Rewari says that children should be taught to save money as early as possible. She feels that parents should teach them the value of money early in life…make them understand that one needs to work hard for it and that it doesn't grow on trees. Towards the end of the month, you may have a financial crunch. Just be open to them about it so that they understand that things don't come easy.

She advises that a joint bank account should be opened with them to create a sense of pride for a child that comes with holding an account. At the same time, they should be taught how a bank functions: give them real-life experiences by taking them to the bank and introducing them to transactions, filling in slips, etc. Give them a monthly allowance and see how they spend it, and mention the reasons for giving them the allowance. Give them money to buy things for the house. See if they are doing the calculations correctly.

10. Leadership

Shah says that to prepare future leaders, children should be taught to see a problem as a challenge. It is about 'blooming wherever you are planted' and making the most of your resources. A good leader should know the difference between wants and needs, and learn to prioritize accordingly. She adds that one must not act impulsively, and that doing what is right, even when no one is watching, is an important trait of a leader. This is a trait that needs to be developed in children.

Dr Marker suggests that leadership skills teach a child communication and give them self-confidence. If a child cannot accept and tolerate people, irrespective of gender, class, sexual orientation, race or disability, then it is the responsibility of parents and schools to help the child to be tolerant.

11. Time management

Estimating the time needed for something, doing tasks on time, being on time, thinking of an idea that is relevant to our time are all part of time management, which is an important life skill. Giving children a visual estimate of time is important so that they can keep track of it for any activity. Sand timers are good for young children who cannot read time on a clock. Learning how to see the time is a complex thing for children. Making them pick up the skill of time management through a sand timer is the best way, as it provides strong visual understanding.

Benefits of life skills

Now that you have read about the most important life skills, let us see how they actually help your child.

Life skills help in:
- **Developing identity and self-expression**: They help children develop and understand themselves better
- **Developing confidence**: They help promote self-esteem

✳ **Developing social skills:** They help children understand and accept others who may be very different from them

✳ **Cultivating dependability:** They help in good decision-making and problem-solving by enabling children to explore all their available alternatives and get to know the various consequences of their actions

✳ **Cultivating independence**: They help children learn to think rationally and logically and not be dependent on others

✳ **Managing emotions**: They help children learn to handle emotions such as anger, grief and melancholy

✳ **Developing time consciousness:** They teach children to value their time and then they are likely to value the time of others and earn the goodwill of their peers

Children who play more do better in life

Child psychologists have said that children who play more outdoor games do better in life, and it makes them smarter too. Less structured activities like playing hide-and-go-seek in the park, climbing trees and visiting the zoo can lead to better performance from an academic point of view. Routine activities can dampen a child's ability to think freely.

Playing or being outdoors lets the child be a child. Every child needs that playtime where they can imagine freely. Sports help children grasp concepts better. Moreover, playing ensures fitness, teamwork, discipline and tunes the mind to think critically. Outdoor play is a multi-sensory activity.

Children who are more involved in activities that are not structured per se will do better in academics, as they are capable of setting their own targets and are much more flexible when it comes to switching between activities. They are capable enough to take charge of their lives and control their moods. Children who play are fitter, happier, more competitive in a healthy way and fall sick less frequently. Children who love sports are honest and sporting, their sense of concentration is higher and they are better able to deal with hardships in life. Playing, whether a professional sport or a hobby, is an important part of motor skill development and hand-eye coordination. Besides intellectual development, you will also find that people who play a sport are more disciplined and focused, and they have a drive.

Unscheduled and unsupervised playtime is what parents can gift to their children for their independent upbringing. My friend and psychologist, Seema Hingorrany, mentioned that playing is known to be very therapeutic. It has a positive impact on the brain, increasing the amount of feel-good hormones. Children learn to be gregarious, and they are able to enhance their social skills by playing.

Children who play are known to have better attention spans, as they learn to multitask better. Their focus is much better compared to children who do not play. These children learn to do their own jobs much earlier in life, for instance, tying their own shoelaces, getting ready for school and even ironing their own clothes when they are in senior school.

Some psychologists also believe that children who play more have better social skills too.

It is at the playground that children strengthen social bonds and build emotional maturity. Playing involves interactions with peer groups, which enhances social development skills.

Children who play with other children and have a big

circle of friends have better social skills. They are much more adaptable and they learn to take their own decisions and solve their own problems. They get along with their peers better as equals rather than as their subordinates. They learn to fight for themselves early in life.

Parents should grant their children some free time to just play some unstructured game, do some imaginary landscape painting or read a fairy tale rather than dictating them to play some carefully planned educational game. Free play is nature's way of teaching children that they can take care of themselves and that they are not alone and helpless. Unstructured activities make children confident and prepare them for the future when they can take risks in life.

The social skill set includes team-building, the ability to cooperate with others, especially in team sports, adaptation to groups and communication skills which they need in order to engage actively with one another.

5

Know Your Style of Parenting

ach parent is different, and the approach they take has an influence on the personality of the child. I know of some parents who go through the belongings of their children, be it books, school bags, or cupboards, and install CCTV cameras to see whether the child is studying or not. I have also looked through my son's belongings, not knowing that while it is my duty to keep a check on my child, doing so for every little thing can hamper his development. Avoid encroaching upon the privacy of your children. Teenagers, especially, need their privacy. Parents should emphasize on helping children develop their life skills and try to be a guide to them so that they grow up to be happy, independent and responsible human beings.

There are several styles of parenting and you can find out which one you have adopted from the list below.

1. Tiger parenting

A term coined by Yale Law School professor, Amy Chua, tiger parents are those who are always hovering around their children, deciding what they should or should not do. The child of a tiger parent cannot watch a movie, use the computer for anything but studies or call over friends unless approved by the parents. It is an extreme case of authoritarian parenting. The children may be successful during the initial years of their lives because parents are helping them out in every step and ensuring that things are done perfectly, whether it is homework or a school project, but in the long run they might fail miserably. When children of tiger parents leave their homes for college, they are unable to manage things on their own because they have always been protected by their parents. When a friend's elder son left home to study commerce at a college in a different city, he couldn't cope with the stress of doing things on his own and studying at the same time. He was so used to his parents making timetables for him and helping him with his revision, that, in college, when he was left to do things on his own, he failed in his first semester. That was a big blow for him as well as his parents.

2. Jellyfish parenting

This term of parenting was coined by Shimi Kang in the magazine *Psychology Today*. This is exactly the opposite of tiger parenting. Jellyfish parents are overly lenient. The parents are happy-go-lucky ones who don't like to bother their children at all with studies and other activities. These children may appear to be very smart and confident, but they are likely to lack direction. Since their parents do not guide them, they are generally academically weak. They are not willing to take life seriously, lack discipline and are not willing to follow any rules. These children may become easy victims of drugs and alcohol.

3. Dolphin parenting

The most balanced and ideal form of parenting, this allows firmness and flexibility at the same time. Children are guided in the right direction and given advice as and when required. These parents create a healthy atmosphere for their children's development, and the children of such parents grow up to be healthy and independent adults who can take charge of their lives.

Be a hands-on parent

From my own experience I have seen that being a hands-on parent helps create a better emotional connection with your child. Research from Columbia University-based National Center on Addiction and Substance Abuse published in their digital magazine stated that parents who take a hands-on approach to raising their children not only have a better relationship with their children, but these children also have fewer chances of getting addicted to drugs or alcohol.[2]

---

[2] John Muturi, 'What it means to be a hands-on parent,' Eve Woman, 15 August 2016, https://www.standardmedia.co.ke/evewoman/article/2000212105/what-it-meansto-be-a-hands-on-parent

Healthy food can't be force-fed

Walking the tightrope begins at an early stage. For instance, your child will grow up to be a healthy adult only if as parents you have guided them to make the right nutritious choices from the time they were toddlers. Try to set an example by inculcating good dietary habits, like teaching them to have a balanced diet with the correct portion of fruits, vegetables, proteins and carbs. You can also take the child on trips to the market and in picking up the correct vegetables and fruits. I used to do this with my son when he was around three years old, and that is how he learnt all the names of fruits and vegetables as a child and also their nutritional values. Instead of force-feeding your child to eat healthy, make them understand why it is important to eat healthy. And also make them understand that healthy food can be delicious too. Just tell them that they are not going to grow up tall and stout like their father or any hero that they admire, like Captain America for instance, if they don't eat healthy food. Try and make healthy food tasty and discourage them from being a picky eater.

Read with your child

If you want to steer your child away from gadgets, it is necessary to consciously inculcate the habit of reading in them. From the time a child develops eyesight and hearing, you can start with showing them pictures of books and reading out stories to them. This habit can be started even before a child learns to read. If you are reading about animals, mimic the sounds to make them feel engaged. Start off with activity books and simple pop-up story books. Then gradually move to stories by Enid Blyton when they are able to read sentences properly, by the time they are six years old. A part of a room in your house can become a reading corner. You can also encourage the child to use new words in regular conversations. If there is a moral in a story, then ask them what it means. Encourage a child to be emotional and understand the story and analyse every character of the particular story. Ask them what their favourite character is and why they are so fond of that particular character.

Screen time

We all know that gadgets have become an important part of our modern-day lives. The best way to keep children away from them is by the parent staying active. Research shows that too much gaming can lead to depression, behavioural issues and obesity in children. Screen time should be limited to not more than one hour in a day for middle-school children, and they should be engaged in outdoor activities that also help strengthen the immune system. Padma Rewari, my dear friend, said that being indoors all the time can also create health issues for children. Hours spent on games can trigger hyperactivity in children. We cannot completely wean off the present lifestyle, but to bring in balance in our lives is certainly in our hands. Children are unable to cope with stress because there is no real outlet.

If a child sees an inactive parent, they start aping them. If a child sees a parent who is active, they get inspired by their habits. Be a role model for your child. Take children outdoors, not just to the mall but for nature walks, for a swim, a game of football, tennis or to the park. What they see is what they do. What do you think a child will do if they see their parent browsing social media every five minutes? Rewari said that she had children coming to her and complaining that their parents don't even look in their direction when they are having a conversation; they are stuck to their mobile phones. It is true that in today's world, you cannot do without technology, but parents should seriously think about spending quality time with their children, without any gadgets.

Scientifically, we don't even know what infrared radiation can do to us. We are just dabbling with the side effects of technology. Since we cannot do without gadgets, we should be mindful of screen time. And once we as parents make a conscious effort, everything will fall into place. It is more of a parenting issue than a child's issue which needs to be corrected.

As mentioned earlier, it is also important to teach children the value of money early in their lives. You must show them that money doesn't grow on trees and that we really need to work hard for it. For a very long time, my son used to think that money comes from an ATM. To correct that, I took the pain of making him understand the entire process of banking and how we need to save a little all the time from our income. Start by buying your child a piggy bank and let them save a little money every day. Assign them jobs like making the bed, laying the table, helping you in grocery shopping and, in return, give them some pocket money. This will make them understand that one needs to work to get money. Board games like Monopoly and Game of Life can also help them learn about money.

Since parenting is a team effort, involve the grandparents, siblings, aunts, uncles and cousins in the child's development. Outings with family and friends can help them see the importance of love and also help them to socialize with others.

Stress management for parents

Parental expectations not only cause stress to children but also to parents. We don't want to judge our children's actual abilities when it comes to academics, and we all have the feeling that our children should stand out in a crowd. We should remember that every child has a unique ability to be different from others.

Our expectations from our children's academic abilities,

even more than their physical abilities, are typically very high. Not only do we overestimate our child's abilities, we like to control their lives, even when the child is a pre-schooler. We decide their wake-up time, meal time, playtime and sleep time. We are so concerned about competition that we end up deciding their schedules and their direction in life right from the time they are born, and when the child is unable to live up to our expectations, we get stressed.

From the time the child is born or maybe even before that, parents tend to make targets. We keep telling ourselves, 'This is where my child is going to do his schooling, then college, then jobs and finally, marriage…this is the kind of spouse I want for my child.' When we create a target, a huge fear lurks at the back of our mind: what if my child is unable to achieve the set targets? Do I have a backup plan? The spiral of expectation rises higher and higher. This leads to stress, which not only pull us down but also severely damages the self-esteem of the child in the long run. But unfortunately, most parents are unaware of this. If you have ever slapped your child because they did not obey you (they slept too late, for instance), you know what I am talking about. It starts from this and the end is yet to come. We start scheduling their lives slowly, thinking that we are guiding them, and end up controlling them.

Chances are that the child, after sometime, may grow up to be a diffident one who will be unable to take any kind of pressure. They may also turn out to be an extremely stubborn child who will resist everything you say. If you are experiencing this resistance from your child, ask yourself if you have unconsciously crossed the line. Overparenting can get torturous for the children and sometimes they might end up feeling that they have no control over their choices, and that the remote control of their life is in the hands of their parents.

We, as parents, need to be patient and inch towards success gradually. If your child is lagging behind in a certain subject, just give them the time. A little change in the way you treat them will make a lot of difference. Say, for instance, your child is weak in Maths and doesn't find the subject interesting at all. Tell them you will sit down and do Maths together and make it fun. The same goes for reading a lesson or learning spellings; turn it into a fun activity. A little change in your way of dealing with your children can make a lot of difference. Try and be low-key instead of hovering about them all the time. For example, as a new mother, you may be sometimes puzzled about what the right time for your child to sleep is, and it is natural to be that way. You are new parents, and understanding your child's requirement takes time. The child too takes time to settle down. If you are nervous and puzzled, your child is likely to be affected by that and feel stressed. Try to make bedtime fun by playing with some rattles on the bed, showing them pop-up story books and reading to them.

6

Smart Ways to Let Go

Letting go as a parent is easier said than done. As children grow up and plan to leave the nest for higher studies, parents suddenly feel an emptiness in their lives. For mothers, it's like their umbilical cord being torn again. They start suffering from the empty nest syndrome. The notion of letting go can create a level of anxiety most parents cannot prepare for.

We, as mothers, also go through phases of turmoil when we have to stop breastfeeding, stay away from our children for a few hours when they start going to playschool followed by nursery school, and then when the child grows up and leaves school for college and higher studies. It is easier said than done to just let go. Until and unless we are going through it, it is very difficult to understand. Only when we are put in a similar situation, do we realize the storm that is raging inside us, to be separated from our children. It is the most difficult tug-of-war for parents to let go. Talk to yourself. For instance, when your children begins to grow up, you will have to stop breastfeeding, send them to school, and then to another city or country for higher studies. It is not for anybody else but your own child's well-being. And if you want to see your child become a happy, independent and successful young person, try to wean yourself from the children first. Remember, letting go of the attachment helps boost the child's development.

If you don't want to go through the hard shock of sudden separation from your children, the best thing is to take baby steps.

- A few months before you send your child to playschool, start by leaving them for one hour initially in the hands of a reliable babysitter or a relative or friend who is happy to help. You can keep a watch over them, or if you are leaving them in the park with the nanny, take your evening rounds in and around the park. This way, their social skills will also improve.

✖ In their pre-teen and teenage years, try to send your child to summer camp or a trekking expedition. This will give them an exposure to life without you and at the same time, you will also learn to live without them.

✖ Take out some time for yourself that is exclusively 'me time'. Don't feel guilty because you can never pour from an empty cup. You need to take care of yourself to take care of your family.

Once you stop overparenting, you will realize that you have started to live your life and you are letting others live their lives too. As mothers, we always tend to put ourselves last. We ignore our health, our passions. And we start living not for ourselves, but for others. You want to be a perfect mother, but that is not possible.

I like to think of myself as a bohemian mother, who loves to travel and play outdoors with her son. Being a mother can never stop me from leading a free-spirited life. Be eccentric, have a quirky sense of style and most importantly, be you. Anyone who says motherhood is easy clearly isn't doing it right. Jokes apart, well, practically, yes, it isn't a five-finger exercise, but having the right approach, energy and attitude towards life can make the journey fun and worthwhile. A boho mother first needs to be comfortable with herself, only then can she teach her child to be happy-go-lucky. It is the happiness and vibrancy of a boho mother that is infectious.

The boho spirit is not limited to a way of dressing or fashion sensibility; it instead is a way of life where you nurture your children with a humble way of life with absolutely no pressure of meeting a set social standard. It encourages freedom of expression and the ability to live life freely and happily.

Motherhood is an exercise in faith, an endless race of the heart and a living testimony of resilience, not some conventional, controlled way of living. What keeps me euphorically strong is my bohemian spirit.

7

At Home with Nature

Gone are the days when children used to play hide-and-go-seek, climb trees, build sand castles and get dirty in the mud. Nowadays, fun for them means being glued to the screen. Nature is an essential part of our well-being, and children today are not connected to it as they should be. It is important to make our children understand that loving nature means protecting it, and each one of us should do our bit.

As parents we have to see if we are providing the right

environment for the overall development of the child, which includes mental health and well-being. The family plays an important role in creating a real environment to nurture the young mind, and this can happen only if we consciously spend time with nature.

Dr Swati Popat Vats, President, Podar Education Trust, pointed out to me that nature takes care of us in so many ways; it feeds us, gives us water and provides for our basic needs. And yet we end up abusing it, knowingly and unknowingly. It is time we teach children to fall in love with nature. When you love something, you will always take care of it as though it belongs to you. Robert Louv in his book, *Last Child in the Woods,* wrote strongly about 'nature deficit disorder'. Experts say that closeness to nature helps to develop physical, intellectual, emotional and social skills in children.

1. Play and get dirty

Parents are wired to be protective, but often we become overprotective. 'Don't play in the sun', 'Don't touch that tree', 'Don't play in the grass, you will get dirty' or the common, 'Go and play, but please don't come back in dirty clothes' are things we say to our children while scolding them. On one hand, adults teach children that nature is dirty and unhealthy, and ask them to stay away from it, and on the other hand, they try to teach the same children to 'save nature' and 'save the trees'. These might confuse the child. We need the calming connect with nature and should allow children to spend considerable time in the lap of nature.

Spending time with nature means rumble-tumble dirty play for children. Let the child get dirty on the beach, allow them to get drenched in the rain and let them splash water in the puddle. Dr Marker said in an interview to me, 'Parents should stop taking out the sanitizer. Immunity can be built up by exposure. The more you expose the child to mud and dirt, the better the immunity.'

2. Nurture the senses

Help children use their senses to explore and experience nature. In doing so, they will develop observation skills, build focus and concentration, and at the same time, the sounds, sights and smells of nature will help them in a therapeutic way. Dr Popat says, 'Tell the child to close their eyes as they sit in the park, and tell them to understand the sounds and smells. Talk to them about the sounds of nature and whatever appeals to their senses the most. If you take your children to a beach, allow them to feel the waves and the sand. Let them search for seashells.'

3. Adopt a tree

Let your child choose a plant or a tree and adopt it, take care of it, water it, name it and nurture it. Dr Popat says, 'You will see an immediate change in your child when you let a tree belong to them, i.e. the power of belonging. This will help instil a sense of leadership and responsibility in children. Ask your child, 'Is anyone hurting or harming your tree?' or 'Who lives in your tree?' Also make children aware about not plucking leaves, as they are the food factory of a tree.

Gardening can be one way to speak to your child about nature and make them understand what is happening, and this is also one way of spending quality time with your children. Plant a tree with your child and help them observe the growth of that plant from a sapling to a tree. Teach them to take care of the plant. They will learn to be more caring and responsible and will have something to look forward to. This will teach them the very important lesson that plants take their own time to grow. Gardening requires patience, which children are losing today due to instant gratification through the Internet. We can all keep a few potted plants in the balcony and grow lemons, chillies, tomatoes and brinjals in our own little kitchen garden. Involve the children in watering the plants and making compost. Teach them about recycling, reusing and reinventing.

4. Make bird feeders

Help your child make simple bird feeders and then watch the birds that come to your balcony for food, discuss their shape, size, colour and sounds. Dr Anjali Chhabria, Mumbai-based renowned psychiatrist and author of *Death is Not an Answer: Understanding Suicide and Ways to Prevent It*, once told me, 'Animals and birds are a part of nature. When you show respect and love towards them, the happiness that you get in return cannot be counted. I would suggest that you choose adoption over buying a pet. And the second thing is that if you cannot have an animal in the house, just adopt a stray in your building and take care of them by feeding them on time and teaching your child to take care of their health. Just keep a tub of water on your windowsill and bird food like vegetable and fruit peel. To see different birds coming and bathing and drinking water is so captivating that children don't really need any toys to play with.'

Share information with your child and ask them questions to arouse their curiosity—'Did you know that a male sparrow has a black band around the neck? Do other birds have gender differentiators too? What about animals?'

5. Encourage outdoor activities

'Outdoor activities like trekking, sports and running around and playing hide-and-go-seek actually enhance the emotional, psychological and social well-being of children of all age groups,' says Dr Marker. Outdoor activities and team sports encourage the social skills of children. Take children for nature walks and discuss the different types of trees and leaves and their different shapes. Mumbai-based clinical psychologist, Dr Varkha Chulani, says, 'Racquet games like tennis, squash and badminton help children develop focus, agility, flexibility and reaction time.'

6. Plan trips to the park

Dr Pervin Dadachanji, Mumbai-based psychiatrist, says that we should take our children to the park instead of a mall. Stop to admire the flowers with bees buzzing around them. Point to a bird making a nest on the branch of a tree. On holidays, incorporate a walk to the park. Every single day children must go outdoors to play. If there is a park close by, it is worth the effort to take them there. Greenery is very soothing and healthy for the development of children. Allow them to play with mud, climb trees and do things that you did when you were young.

Going close to nature stimulates creativity and imagination. It helps children think out of the box. Some of the best artists' and poets' creations are nature-based. Nature has its own beautiful ways to calm a child. It is also an excellent teacher of anger management.

7. Nature-friendly holidays

Spend a holiday in a natural environment with the entire family. My recommendation to parents is that they should take the children to a game reserve every year: just that atmosphere of being one with animals in their natural habitat with no Wi-Fi is a sure way of spurring children to connect with nature. Once they have experienced it first-hand, it is easier for them to want more nature-friendly outings. It is important that parents talk to their children about the environment and their role in saving it.

8

Digital Detox

Computer addiction can be just as powerful as drug addiction. According to an article in *The Telegraph*[3], UK, a Chinese teenager was rushed to hospital after he took a drastic measure and cut off his own hand in an attempt to cure his Internet addiction. Back home, lots of children have digital addiction. Let's take a look at the ways

---

[3]Tom Phillips, 'Chinese teen chops hand off to "cure" internet addiction,' *The Telegraph*, 3 February 2015. Available at https://www.telegraph.co.uk/news/worldnews/asia/china/11386325/Chinese-teen-chops-hand-off-to-cure-internet-addiction.html

to keep your child away from the computer.

1. Have you talked about it?

Find out if there are any specific reasons that a child spends so much time on the computer. Sometimes, the computer acts as an escape from reality. If your child is facing problems that are causing a desire within them to 'escape', try and address those. Teach your child to share their feelings and emotions with real people like friends and family, rather than suppressing them and sharing them with unknown people they meet on social media.

2. Where do you keep the computer?

Keeping the computer in a separate room is enough to reduce its usage by your child. But always observe what they are accessing. That way it becomes easy to monitor the amount of time the child spends in front of the screen.

3. How many gadgets does your child have?

Avoid giving your child all the gadgets you have. If you feel sorry for your children, you are likely to indulge them, which can worsen the addictions.

4. Are you denying anything?

It is important for the parent to admit that the child is addicted to the computer. Find out what they are addicted to on the computer: social media, playing games, browsing the net, going to porn sites or chatting with friends and strangers.

5. Can you filter access without censoring?

If your child is gathering information that is useful to their education, then they should be appreciated for it. Whenever parents come to me with problems of children spending too much time in front of the computer, I tell them that they need to see what the children are doing on the net, and if it is something educational, then they should be encouraged. But if they are just socializing and wasting time, then parents need to be alert. If children spend more than an hour on social media, then it is time to talk to them about time limits.

6. Is there a time limit?

See to it that your child sticks to the time limit. Make a conscious effort to list how many hours your child is spending online and then slowly start reducing the hours.

It has been observed that this hardly works, since they don't realize how time flies in front of the computer. I keep a timer and once it goes off, my son has to get off the computer. This should apply for adults as well, and parents should set a good example for children by not playing Candy Crush as the child does their homework.

7. Encourage outdoor activities

Replace the time that your child spends in front of the computer with some fun outdoor activities. Indulging in outdoor activities such as trekking, walking on the beach or in the garden and being close to nature will provide the much-needed break from the muddled-up thoughts that increase online addiction.

8. Spend time with your child

It is important to know if your child is suffering from deep loneliness, as such people are hooked on to the Internet, and they seek instant gratification for their feelings and emotions there. Such children are legitimately lonely, so the computer becomes a place for social contact. Sit with your child and spend some quality time together. Play board games with them or read out a book.

9. Do they have hobbies?

Help your child develop a hobby or a skill like swimming or baking. This will take their mind off the screen, and at the same time, be relaxing and therapeutic.

10. When to take the computer away

Addictions are hard to break and sometimes it becomes important to take the computer away completely. Remove its power cord. If there is more than one computer in the house, it is important to find out if they are using them secretively. Take a look at the Internet browsing history to find out if there is any site that has not been used by you.

Practise what you preach

When I was young, my parents and others from their generation used to rely primarily on instinct to take care of our needs. The new parents of today are mostly technologically advanced, some of them millennials, and their access to technology has brought about a change in parenting. Inevitably, children are also affected by it.

They are probably the most competitive as parents

and some of them have taken on parenting as a full-time job. And unlike previous generations, they are more open-minded. That we should feel glad to have information easily available on the net is stating the obvious. The fact remains that millennials as parents have to face challenges too.

The influence of social media is huge in a parent's life. From the first solid food tasting to potty training, there are updates about the tiniest aspect of our child's growth. We have various mommy groups on social media where one can discuss parenting and food habits, and mothers also share what to give a child as their first solid food. There are times mothers share recipes to give a healthy twist to junk food by bringing about a few wise changes in the ingredients, keeping the taste intact. Support groups for new mothers, for instance, allow them a free space to share their concerns and happiness that may not have been possible otherwise.

But do we wonder if and how social media has influenced our style of parenting? Parents need to be aware about how their use of social media can affect their children psychologically. Our children are likely to have an opinion and get influenced by our need to 'like' and 'share' incessantly on social media. While it is good to seek advice about health and education, parents forget that the Internet is full of unverifiable content. Another problem is that sharing unnecessary information that can get into the wrong hands, such as paedophiles, can lead to grave dangers. Think about the pictures you upload and the messages you convey through them. Your child is likely to see them sooner or later, and you don't want to send out the wrong message to them. Most importantly, keep in mind your child's security, cyber and real.

How to be mindful on social media

When we try to teach our children how to use social media responsibly, we should be careful about what we are doing. We talk to our children about how there are certain things that should stay only within the family. We teach them that it is bad to flaunt our achievements. But as adults we end up doing the same things.

Not only do we brag about our own achievements, but we end up sharing things about our children unnecessarily too. From the time the child is born till the first word they utter, and then their big achievements, we want to put up everything on social media. It's time that parents should think things through before they post pictures or other details of their children on social media.

One of my very close friends who was pretty active on social media recently had a baby. But I was surprised that she did not even post a single picture of her newborn child. Another friend of mine also makes a conscious effort not to post too many pictures of her son and his achievements on social media. She explained that she wants her son to be able to choose whether he wishes to be on social media or not, and it is up to him to decide about his social media identity.

Avoid scripting your child's achievements on social media. If you want to remember each and every phase of your child's development, then maintain a diary. It is not that you shouldn't post anything about children on social media, but one needs to be careful about what they post, just the way they advise their teenage children to be careful on social media.

9

Coping with Failure

When you fail an exam, it isn't easy to handle the failure. But remember that even the greatest minds have suffered setbacks in their lives, and it is normal to fail. Here are a few ways in which children can cope with exam failures and parents can support them.

1. Learn from failure

Learning from failure helps you see a positive path. Take a step back and weigh your options. See if you can retake the exam and bring up your grades. Find out ways to improve in the subjects you have flunked. Academics are only one facet of life, and marks don't define anybody. It is not the end of life, and one setback does not define you. Success in life is not dependent on how much you score in exams. A combination of things makes you successful. Failure can happen because of various reasons and the best way to tackle it would be to unearth the reason.

2. Talk it out

Withdrawing into a shell is the worst thing that a child can do. It may sound difficult, but it is important that they talk it out with their close friend. The support of family and friends will help them to overcome their tough times. Help them find out where they went wrong, as that will help them prepare better for their next exam. Look online for forums where students in the same situation share their worries and share this with your child, as this will calm them and do wonders for their confidence.

3. Stay focused

The pressure to pass exams can bombard your child from all sides. Your children have expectations to meet, and perform well for themselves too. When they flunk, the pressure to do well in the next exam increases manifold. But, as parents, it is time for us to take a call and help them to stay focused. When they sit for the re-exam, keep realistic goals. Tell your children to ask their teachers about their drawbacks and work on them accordingly.

4. Don't linger

It is not possible that the journey will be smooth all the time. Moving on in life is what is important. Dwelling on setbacks isn't going to make them go away. Accept them and help your child accept them and make peace with what has happened. Mulling and brooding over failure will not change anything. Children should ask themselves what they need to do to help themselves move forward.

5. Think of inspirational figures

No one achieves success without failures and challenges. Role models help. However, children should not try to emulate anyone completely. They should take the best traits from people and build a unique identity for themselves.

6. Bounce back

A rubber ball has the ability to bounce back—it has resilience. People develop resilience and tenacity when they don't get devastated by defeat. If you don't want your child to feel low all the time, then don't let despair and failure bother them. In order to help them come out of the state of depression, encourage them to think about the long term and their aspirations.

10

Money and Looks

Children today care too much about material possessions. They think money can buy everything and that it grows on trees. I remember my husband went on foreign deputation for two years and I had to bring up my child, who was then not even five years old, single-handedly. My son asked me, 'Mama, why don't I get a toy from you every month?' I told him, 'Baby, money doesn't grow on trees and you need to work really hard to make a comfortable living for yourself and your family.' My barely five-year-old son said, 'Go to the ATM and you will get money.' For him, it was like shaking a tree: you just need to shake it hard for money to fall into your hand. I made him understand that money doesn't grow on trees.

My question is, does your child always want to buy the latest PlayStation, computer games, electronic toys, gadgets, dolls, designer clothes and CDs? Does your nine-year-old want to treat their friends at a high-end restaurant on their birthday? And do you, as a parent, always give in to their wants? Have you ever realized that you could be raising a child for whom owning the latest gadgets is the key to being accepted among peers? Today, children are being overpowered by mass media because of which they need to project a certain image of themselves to their peers. But the best of clothes, toys and gadgets will not make them happier or more happening. Longer working hours for parents, more academic and extracurricular demands from children and lesser family time have resulted in parents feeling guilty about not giving enough to their children. They often try to make up for their reduced availability by giving material gifts to children and going easy on them when it comes to discipline.

While children and teens are under tremendous pressure to acquire all those tempting toys or gadgets available, parents are under equally great pressure to buy it for them. Many parents find it difficult to say 'no' to their children. It is easier to give in and get them what they ask for than having to explain why the child won't get what they want. This seems to be especially true for parents who don't deny themselves anything. And when a thirteen-year-old comes home from their friend's sprawling house, in which the bedroom is complete with a complex stereo system, TV, phone with a private number, a walk-in closet and a computer with Internet access, they are less than satisfied with their smaller bedroom that contains far fewer accessories. It is important for parents to instil positive values in their children when they are young and send the message that money can't buy love and the most beautiful things in the world.

From an early age, children see their parents using the ATM, writing cheques and paying by credit card. So, they think that their parents have a lot of money to spend. You have to explain money basics in an age-appropriate manner. As parents, it is important for us to tell our children that you earn money by working hard, and it is important not to squander it.

I remember that I used to explain to my son that the bank is like a giant piggy bank. 'Mommy and Daddy put money in when they get paid for their jobs, and not by sitting and whiling away time. When we need some, we only take out a little. But we make sure that our piggy bank never gets empty. In the same way, when you put money into your piggy bank, you need to save it just the way Mommy and Daddy do. So be careful with money and spend wisely. If it finishes, you are not going to get more. If today you waste money on things that you don't need, then tomorrow a day might come when you will not have money to buy things that you need.

Advertisements have a strong influence on children. Your child might get the hang of managing money early if you explain to them how advertising can make you want things you don't really need or can't really afford. Tell them that the purpose of advertisements is to get people interested in buying products, not to entertain the viewer or reader. Talk about the ways in which a product is made attractive on the television screen or the social media or magazine page…the colour used, the packaging, the display and so on.

It is not easy in our hectic lives to give children the time and attention they crave. If the parents are always busy, then the children will retreat to their toys and TV and cartoons, and all kinds of other material attractions. Children have to have a family life to replace that. As parents, we should try not to give our children things as a substitute. And we should make an effort to spend time together doing things that don't cost anything: go to the playground and the library and take nature walks. No matter what your child says they want and need, the security, comfort and support that the family can provide is more important than a room full of possessions, and your child needs to understand that.

We all live in very hard times, and making both ends meet is not an easy task. Everybody needs to be careful with money. If you see that peer pressure is contributing to your child's materialistic streaks, teach them assertive skills like saying 'no', and help them counter the pressure. The more children understand about budgeting, where the money really goes and their own roles in the family, the less likely they are to make extravagant demands to keep up with peers.

You cannot equate love with money. If you can take the

time and make the effort to plant the seeds of contentment and gratitude in your children and nurture them through the years, you will be giving them something far greater and more useful than any material possession!

Five mistakes to avoid when you talk about money

In order to make their children value money, parents often end up talking down to them, and fail to make an impact. Let's look at the five mistakes they end up committing when it comes to money matters and children.

1. Bribing children to get good grades

Most parents have a habit of bribing their children when it comes to grades, not realizing the harmful effect it has on them. They should instead explain to the children the importance of education, and how a lack of good education could affect their future. The motivation to do well in studies or any extra-curricular activities should come from within. And this realization that they are studying for their own good should also come early.

2. Giving children pocket money for household chores

Chores are a part of the discipline during the developmental phases of your child's life. It helps them to be responsible, and also, helpful. Allowances for getting them to do their chores can be the worst thing a parent could do. Stress on the importance of diligence and conscientiousness by narrating real incidents and stories of real people. Psychologist Seema Hingorrany says that paying allowances to children for doing household chores causes confusion and gives rise to unreasonable expectations in their mind. This may also be harmful when they grow up to be a young adult, where they feel that chores are a job, not their duty.

3. Not talking about money with children

If you don't talk to your children about money matters early in your life, they will not value it at all. Empowering children by teaching them to adopt good money-minding habits in their formative years is one of the greatest gifts a parent can give to them. Your financial standing should be clearly explained to them during the initial years of growing up.

We all agree that branding has caught on in a big way in India. Today, children decide which brand of cheese and jam they prefer. The influence of a peer group also makes it very difficult for children to be careful with money. Like so many other aspects of everyday life, the way we save, spend, account for and think about money also becomes a habit.

Parents should try and introduce the concept of saving money to children step by step, befitting the child's age and understanding. A child's expectations can only keep escalating if they are made to dwell in a make-believe world. You, as parents, should know where to draw the line.

4. Teaching only sons about money

'In the twenty first century, both the genders are successful in their respective fields of work. Women are venturing out to carve a niche for themselves. Many girls today are studying aboard, trying to fend for themselves financially,' says Hingorrany. She adds that both the genders, hence, need finance education and tips on money concepts, and parents should pay heed to that.

Good looks don't make a child happy

Children, especially little girls, like to ape their mothers. I have seen little girls getting pampered from head to toe, indulging in manicure, pedicure and facials. Considering that we live in such a looks-obsessed society, is it right to get them hooked on beauty regimes at a young age? The pressure to look good is high. I remember one of my friends mentioning how her daughter had come home from school crying, because her teacher had told her to stand in the last row during dance performance because she was dark. You can't blame kids for being sensitive in such cases because the treatment they receive at the hands of narrow-minded adults is not fair.

The other day, another friend of mine was talking about her ten-year-old daughter. She mentioned to me in a chat, 'Though I don't allow my daughter to thread or wax, she is very particular about the way she looks. Whenever I take her to the beauty parlour for a haircut, she decides what cut she wants. She has developed a mind of her own at a very young age.'

Botox is becoming very popular among teenagers. They're hearing about it from their mothers, so it trickles down. A cosmetic surgeon once told me, 'We have had a girl walking in with a picture of her mother and say, "I don't ever want to have that line like she does." The fourteen-year-old was only copying the seventeen-year-old, who was copying what the mother was doing, and the mother was only forty. If you added up all the ages, maybe that person needed Botox!'

City children are all out to transform themselves. Once they start spending and seeing results, it's hard to make them stop. Like any addiction, it starts with the light stuff. Anika Sharma (name changed to protect her identity), a fourteen-year-old student, gets pocket money for manicures, pedicures and waxing. She's had her hair Japanese-straightened twice ('I need to touch it up!' she says).

Parents should encourage girls to play games and have fun and curb their obsession with looks. Full-body waxing seems benign compared to the more invasive procedures young girls sign up for in anticipation of skirting around the pudgy acne years. A popular dermatologist from Mumbai who doesn't want to be named says that chemical peels and microdermabrasion are standard practices for young patients. Teens even request liposuction under their chin to accentuate the jawline. In the doctor's opinion, the drive for perfection comes from a lack of confidence and the pressure that they face from peers and contemporaries who try and force them to look good all the time. A yoga instructor friend of mine said that a fourteen-year-old girl asked her one day, 'How do I make my abs tight? How can I keep this from jiggling?' Children probably feel better if they are working on themselves and taking their physical idiosyncrasies into their own hands. In many ways, having a 'problem' and quickly fixing it feels good. Often, however, it feels like pressure to be 'perfect' too. With the pressure to look good at all times, everybody wants to be a 'Cosmo girl' overnight!

11

Porn Addiction

Several psychologists I spoke to for a story in *The Times of India* on porn addiction among children said that it is becoming common in India, primarily because of the nuclear family system and the influence of technology. Today, easy access to a vast amount of information and knowledge through the Internet has created a multitude of opportunities for children to access porn. Children have to do a lot of their homework with help from the Internet, and while browsing, there are many instances where random pop-ups of porn sites could arouse the curiosity of the child. In the absence of influential factors such as role models, good company and healthy relationships, this could eventually lead to addiction. Working parents also find it difficult to monitor their child's computer usage. With minimum or no parental guidance, it is increasingly easy for children to visit porn sites, uninterrupted.

A major cause of porn addiction in children is peer pressure. No influence in a teenager's life is as powerful as that of a peer. Peer pressure can impair good judgement and fuel risky behaviour, drawing a child away from the family and its positive influences, and luring them into dangerous activities. The more the child is comfortable with their identity, the less susceptible they will be to peer pressure. Obsessive-compulsive disorders (OCDs) can also lead to porn addiction. It leads to sexual obsessions: unwanted thoughts or images that are upsetting, or interfering with an individual's life, followed by compulsions—actions that temporarily relieve the anxiety caused by the obsessions. Sexual obsessions are involuntary, repetitive and unwelcome. The individual cannot simply wish them away. Attempts to suppress sexual obsessions don't work, and may, in fact, make them more severe.[4]

Exposure to pornography frequently results in sexual addiction, sexual disorders and unplanned pregnancies. As more and more children are exposed, not only to soft pornography but also to explicit sexual material, they are learning an extremely dangerous message from pornographers: *sex without responsibility is acceptable and desirable.* Because pornography encourages sexual expression without responsibility, it endangers children's health as well as their attitudes towards sex. One of the grim consequences of sexual activity among teens has been a steady increase in the extent to which youth are afflicted with venereal diseases. Another obvious result of children getting involved in sexual activity is the increased rate of pregnancy among teenagers.

Another consequence of porn exposure is that children can act out sexually against younger, smaller and more vulnerable children as they tend to imitate what they've seen, read or heard.

---

[4]Lachmi Deb Roy, 'Here's How Kids Become Addicted to Porn', *The Times of India*, 23 October 2015, https://timesofindia.indiatimes.com/life-style/relationships/parenting/Heres-how-kids-become-addicted-to-porn/articleshow/46917604.cms[© Bennett, Coleman & Co. Ltd.]

There is not enough awareness about how porn addiction can interfere with a child's development and identity. It is important to know that getting exposed to healthy sexual norms and attitudes helps in developing a healthy sexual orientation. If the child is exposed to negative sexual attitudes during the time the brain is developing a 'hardwire' for what one will find arousing, sexual deviance can become imprinted on the child's 'hard drive'.

How can parents help?

1. **Be open:** The most important thing for parents to do is to be open about the topics of porn and sex. They should discuss the topic openly with their children. They can ask questions such as: 'Have you ever seen porn?', 'When did you start?' or 'Why do you watch it'? If children are watching porn, parents should not overreact; they should take responsibility for the act and try to figure out solutions.[5]

---

[5]Lachmi Deb Roy, 'Here's how kids become addicted to porn,' *The Times of India*, 23 October 2015, https://timesofindia.indiatimes.com/life-style/relationships/parenting/Heres-how-kids-become-addicted-to-porn/articleshow/46917604.cms [© Bennett, Coleman & Co. Ltd.]

2. **Look for signs**: Parents should check for signs of porn addiction, such as children staying in their locked rooms for a really long time. They should check video games and websites the children are engaging with, and the images featured therein. Increasingly, violent or sexual images are creeping into what parents think are safe sites or games.

3. **Role play**: Parents should show children how to set up personal boundaries with friends when encountering questionable situations, such as sharing sexual images via apps like Snapchat, or texting.

4. **Rule of law**: Explaining consequences of actions to children, such as this—once an image is sent over the Internet, it is not possible to take it back. In some statesin the US, teens caught sexting are now being charged as sex offenders for distribution or possession of child pornography, and some children are even being sent to prison.

5. **Preventive measures**: Take preventive measures by locking your computer, tablets and smartphones with safe browser and Internet filters, so that teens do not get a chance to go to pornography sites, be it accidentally or intentionally.

I wanted to address this topic because I have heard many of my friends complaining about how they have found out, through other people's experience, that children watch porn when their parents are not around. Let me tell you that this can happen in your house as well. But how you deal with it is what is important. Porn addiction in children begins with simple curiosity.

Pornography addiction in children usually starts when they spend too much time in front of the computer, unmonitored. Other circumstances like separation from or of parents, and neglect and abuse also lead children to turn to pornography.

It starts off as curiosity which becomes a habit. When asked, twelve-year-old Reema Sen (name changed) said, 'I started watching porn at the young age of seven when my parents used to go for work and I was alone at home during the holidays. One of my friends told me about certain computer games and there was a pop-up on my computer which showed videos on sex. I was shocked to see the video. When school reopened, I spoke to my friends and they said that they have also seen similar videos. Soon we started sharing videos and I don't know when it became an addiction.'

We all know that in the age of technology, it is extremely difficult to keep children away from computers. If your child is spending excessive time in front of the computer, chances are that they will come across some advertisements which pop up alongside the games (which may not be an adult game), and just a click will take them to the pornography site.

Effect of pornography

Pornography can have an adverse impact on children. Knowing about sex through pornography can damage a young mind and give them an unhealthy idea about sex. When they grow up, they expect their sex life to be similar to the pornography that they watched.

Porn is not damaging in itself. It is how it is used over time that causes damage. A peek, once in a while, at a porn site, is not a problem. It is, when it becomes addictive and leads one to take it as a standard is when it begins to be a problematic situation.

Exposure to porn may also incite children to act out sexually against other children. Children often imitate what they've seen, read or heard.

Pornography interferes with a child's development and identity. During certain critical periods of childhood, a child's brain is naturally programmed for sexual orientation. During this period, the mind appears to be developing a 'hardwire' for what the person will be aroused by or attracted to. Exposure to healthy sexual norms and attitudes during this critical period can result in the child developing a healthy sexual orientation. In contrast, if there is exposure to explicit pornography during this period, sexual deviance may become imprinted on the child's 'hard drive' and become a permanent part of their sexual orientation.

12

Dealing with Special Children

There is a famous African proverb which states that, 'It takes a village to raise a child'. This applies to all children, including special needs children. Often, parents feel lonely on their journey towards raising kids, and with a special needs child, the stress is likely to be more. Staying in denial doesn't help, nor does giving up. Of course, it seems easy to say it, but I want to talk about ways to come out of denial.

It wasn't easy for Pratima Tiwari when her two-year-old

son was diagnosed with autism. The first signs that she noticed were that there was no eye contact when she was having a conversation with him, and the child had some speech issues too. But little did she know that the speech difficulty was due to autism. There are times when having a child with special needs makes you feel that you have been cheated by life. The obvious question that comes to mind is, 'Why me?'

For Pratima, her son Anant looked like any other child of his age. But he behaved differently. Handling the situation correctly was the most difficult part, as for any other parent with special children. Pratima says, 'But at some point, you realize that your child is different and you need to accept it. It can be any disability, but how well parents handle the situation is what matters.'

Viddu Hari, another parent with a special child, was in a similar situation. She got to know that her younger son was autistic when he was around one year old. He used to be completely expressionless and not react to anything. Initially, it was tough for her to cope with the requirements. She used pictures to communicate with him. Her elder son too cooperated a lot in the situation by being extremely caring and protective of his brother.

Living in denial that your child is a special child

There are times when parents spend days, months and even years not accepting that the child has a problem. They continue pretending that everything is fine. The discovery can be a startling change and your plans for life invariably change. Most parents go through depression and they start giving up on life. Often I tell such parents that they need more attention than their special children because they are the primary caregivers. And if they fall sick or are depressed all the time, who is going to take care of the children? I make them feel that they are the chosen ones and that they have it in them to take care of a child with special needs. But for that, they need to take care of themselves first and stop being angry with life.

Denial is not going to help. The first step towards taking care of your child with special needs is acceptance of the harsh reality and living with it in a positive way. Parents of special children need to be realistic, and they should realize that the pace of a special child will not be the same as for any other growing child of their age. They should acknowledge it and not shy away from it.

Detecting disabilities

Understanding 'disability' is very important. When an individual's physical or mental condition has an impact on their daily functioning, i.e. on social interactions, self-care, communication or movements, the condition constitutes a disability. Collaborating with parents via counselling is the most important step when working with any child. Parents are often overwhelmed themselves, so it is important that we take time to understand how they feel about their child's condition, their stress levels, impact of the child's condition on their personal and family life, etc. This understanding is crucial to fostering a supportive environment.

In the case of children with physical disabilities that are apparent, parents can see them and they find it easier to accept. These can be directly seen and it is easier to convince parents to make that extra effort for them. But when there are mental disabilities, parents cannot evaluate them. They feel that the child is facing some issues and will be able to cope once they are old enough. Mental disabilities include subnormality or mental retardation. Parents of children who have very prominent problems find it easier to accept reality, since they can see it. But in cases where the child appears physically normal, but their mental development is mildly hampered, parents often feel that their child is smart, but teachers and the school are being partial.

Once these disabilities are obvious, there are several tests to detect difficulty in reading, writing, concentrating and understanding or even socializing. Sometimes when children suffer from disabilities, they become withdrawn, turn rebellious, disobedient, may lose initiative or show aggression. These problems have to be specifically tackled.

Prachi Deo, who runs an NGO, Nayi Disha Resource Centre, an online information resource platform to empower families of persons with Intellectual or Developmental Disabilities (IDD), told me, 'IDDs are disorders that are usually present at birth and that significantly influence the individual's physical, intellectual and emotional development.' Intellectual disability is characterized by problems with both intellectual functioning and/or intelligence, which includes the ability to learn, reason, solve problems and it also hampers other skills. Affected children have problems in dealing with everyday social and life skills. Some of the common conditions under IDDs are autism spectrum disorder, cerebral palsy and Down syndrome.

Acceptance

Coming to terms with the situation is probably the hardest time any parent will face in their lifetime. Parenthood itself is a very novel experience, with many societal pressures. In the midst of this rollercoaster, to come face-to-face with a situation that is completely alien can give rise to negative emotions. It is normal for parents to go through different stages of emotions, from denial to anger to depression, before coming to terms with the new situation. The key for parents is to get access to as much information as possible, and build a supportive community of family, friends, professionals and other parents who have dealt with similar situations. The idea is to go through the cycle of acceptance as fast as possible so parents can focus on the interventions required for the child.

Focus on the strengths

The best way to deal with special children is to focus on their strengths. The parents of a special child, who refused to be named, said that initially they were sending him to a regular school, but the child was always discriminated against, and was made to sit in a separate place, and they used to get complaints about the child disturbing other children. Although the family understands their needs, the attitude of people towards disabled children is indeed a matter of concern. Not everybody understands that special children need to be given an equal place in society, among all.

What schools can do

Deepa Shetty is the principal of Gopi Birla Memorial School, Mumbai, which specializes in working with students with high/low functioning autism, behavioural issues, learning difficulties as well as students with physical difficulties. She says, 'Disability itself puts a child on the backfoot. In some cases, the child is extremely conscious of being different and incompetent in some way even though it is not their fault. It becomes imperative for the teacher not to complicate things further. Being sensitive and empathetic is important. At the same time, one must not overdo things. Subtle indicators are enough. They should be recognized and appropriately dealt with. Also, the teacher dealing with the child should remember the problems faced by the child and try to make them feel as normal as possible in her dealings with the class as a whole.'

A young friend of mine, Haufrid Billimoria, who is studying for a master's degree in Social Work at the Tata Institute of Social Sciences (TISS), Mumbai, says that people may know a little about disability, but know nothing about dystonia, a rare disease that affects your motor movements because it attacks your neurological system. 'Having severe learning disability was an add-on to my set of challenges. Dystonia affected me when I was fifteen, and it socially drove me into a shell as I was being ragged and bullied just for being different, which I found atrocious. But never did I give up; dystonia had affected my right side completely, and when I was about sixteen years old, I used to limp and walk.'

In spite of all these odds, Haufrid is doing well for himself. Physical fitness helped a lot when he started running and doing hardcore exercises. Of course, it was a gradual process. It was like reminding your muscle memory all that you could do all over again. He got into shape and even his doctors were shocked to see how minimal the involuntary moments had become. Now he can ride a bike, drive a car, do things which any other normal child can. So, remember one thing—one cannot assume what is going to happen in their life, but surely one can change their circumstances with pure grit and willpower.

13

Safe at School

There are a host of conflicting emotions that play within us when we put our children onto the bus or drop them to school. And the recent incidents happening around us make us think about how safe our children are in school. Here is how parents can educate children to be safe in school and the steps that they can take to ensure that their children are safe. There are so many molestations and rapes happening in our country. And sadly, so many cases go unreported.

Awareness in children

You certainly cannot scare your children into not wanting to go to school because of the fear that they might be molested or killed. But at the same time, you don't want to be completely dependent on others, such as school authorities, for protection. So, it makes sense to educate your children about good and bad touch. But at the same time, one must not overburden them with too much information.

Making your child aware of physical abuse should start at home. But that too should be done in a subtle way. Weave it in through communication. Don't make it sound frightening by hitting the panic button. It is time that we, as parents, prepare our children to articulate their problems better. Make the communication interactive, rather than being preachy, and don't overexpose the children to good and bad touch.

Encourage open communication

Good communication between the parent and the child helps to build a bond between them. We need to focus on keeping the environment lively, starting our conversations on a friendly note so that the children are inclined to open up about their dreams, struggles and fears. Always be patient and keep the communication gate open. It is time we parents improve our listening skills. Tell your child that if anybody makes them feel uncomfortable and says any inappropriate thing to them, the child should inform teachers and parents.

Meet the school authorities regularly

The best way to keep in touch with the school's safety policy and follow up with the safety issues is to meet the teachers and the administrators on a regular basis. If the school does not encourage parent-teacher interaction, it is not wise to put your child in that school.

When we leave our children in the hands of the school authority, we assume that the child is in safe hands. We keep the reputation of the school in mind and turn a blind eye towards the rest. Ideally, the school authorities should have a proper check of the employees. They should do a police verification when they are employing everyone and find out if any of the staff has a criminal record. We should check on the first day itself if the school is vigilant towards the entry of strangers. Check the CCTVs and find out if they are operating properly or not; it is a must, according to the CBSE guidelines. But it is sad that seldom do we find them in the appropriate places. And most of the time, they are not functioning properly. If we feel that there has been no background check for a person, then we must bring it to the attention of the higher authorities of the school.

Parents need to be aware of what is happening in school. Though it is not physically possible for them to be there in school, I make it a point to sit with my son the moment I am back home from work. On days when I am not at home, I give him a call to figure out if things are fine at his end. This makes me familiar with what's happening in school and how his day at school has been. No matter how busy we are, both my husband and I make it a point to attend all the PTMs. This, I feel, gives the staff of the school the idea that we take active interest in our child's upbringing.

Dr Swati Popat Vats points out in an interview that as a parent, these are some of the things you can demand from schools.

1. Teachers should be proactive and make regular rounds before the children arrive.

2. Schools should be child-friendly and parent-friendly. If anything goes wrong, the authorities should be approachable.

3. Teachers should give their mobile phone numbers to parents so that they can get in touch with them, and should, at the same time, have the numbers of the parents.

4. Proper background check of the entire staff should be done, with proper police verification.

5. On a monthly basis, an interactive session should be organized in schools. A circular about the child's safety should be sent to the parents on a weekly basis.

6. Life skill classes should be part of the school curriculum.

7. Teachers need to educate children about how to stay safe.

8. Proper survey of the schools should be done by the government on an annual basis.

9. CCTVs should be installed and they should be checked for repair and maintenance.

10. Teachers should stay back for bus duty and there should be lady attendants in school buses.

Parents need to ask children several things to ensure not only that their child is safe but their friends and peers are as well. A proactive parent can help ensure the safety of the school.

Ask your child

1. Have you witnessed any bullying at school?
2. Do you feel safe at school?
3. Does anybody make you feel uncomfortable in school or in the bus?
4. Are you enjoying school?
5. Does any senior in school behave strangely with you?
6. Do you feel respected and wanted by your teachers and classmates?

Safety at home is not guaranteed

Today, children of all ages are being sexually abused. As soon as your child is able to understand about body parts, hands, shoulders, etc., teach them through rhymes and actions about the four body parts that no one can touch except in the presence of parents. If your child is too young to be taught about this, then ensure that they are under 'trusted' adult supervision all the time, even if not with you. Ensure that trust is not blind faith.

Do not kiss your child on the lips, as this only makes them more vulnerable to kisses on the mouth by strangers. Young children then associate this as an acceptable way of showing love.

Avoid threatening your child. When children are regularly threatened, they understand fear and its consequences and are then easy victims of perverts who use threats to intimidate them into not telling you about it.

Never raise your hand on your child. It is normal for parents to then feel guilty about it and hug the child, but this behaviour is then recognized by young children as an acceptable form of showing love and then they accept it from others too. Know whom your child was with and what that person was doing with your child. This is important, as abuse can start with something as insignificant as tickling, touching, fondling, etc. Ask your child often, what games they played with adults and children. When your child describes anything that you feel was not right, like, 'I enjoyed Rahul uncle tickling me and making me sit on his lap,' it should raise a red flag and you should talk to the adult concerned. Never ask your child to hug and kiss someone if they are uncomfortable about it; children have a sixth sense when it comes to such things—trust them. Also, do not refer to everyone as an uncle: doing so makes children think that uncles are safe, so a predator will be an 'uncle'. Instead, refer to uncles with their names—Ajay uncle, etc., so the child knows that only this uncle is safe and not all uncles. If you suspect that someone has abused your child, then confront the person and find out the truth. Do not try to ignore it because you are afraid to 'hurt the other person' or because your 'relationship may suffer'.

Child porn viewing is on the rise, so check the mobile phone video-viewing habits of the people employed by you, especially if they are taking care of or are in contact with your child. Report child sexual abuse, as it will then make the offenders scared about loss of reputation. You not reporting such instances are making them stronger. If you are worried about its impact on your or your child's reputation, ensure that the media or any other reporting authority does not reveal your child's name or your name, according to the Protection of Children from Sexual Offences (POCSO) ACT 2012.

14

Shame, Silence and Sexual Abuse

We should make children aware about sexual abuse at as early as two years of age. Being a working mom most of my life, this was one thing that used to scare me the most. So I started discussing with my son very early in life about right and wrong touch. The discussion at the age of three should be about right and wrong touch. In my opinion, both girls and boys should be taught and made self-aware about sexual abuse. Children at this age do understand various body parts and how nobody should be allowed to touch their private parts.

To discuss child sexual abuse with a child, one need not go into the details of rape. As parents, we should explain abuse from a child's perspective, so that children are empowered, and not scared about the whole thing. It's imperative to keep a check on your own gestures and not make them sound scary to the child, or that the world is filled with bad people. Many children who are very sensitive can develop school phobia if parents don't handle the issue properly.

The following are some signs of abuse

- ✳ Acting in an inappropriate sexual way with toys or objects
- ✳ Nightmares and sleeping problems
- ✳ Becoming withdrawn or very clingy
- ✳ Becoming unusually secretive
- ✳ Sudden unexplained personality changes like mood swings
- ✳ Bedwetting
- ✳ A constant feeling of insecurity

- ✖ Talking about new older friends and gifts of chocolates and toys from them
- ✖ Not wanting to leave the house
- ✖ Soreness and bruises around genitals or mouth

Every parent feels uncomfortable bringing up the topics of sex and sexuality. But you have to address these topics for the benefit of your child. Here is how a parent can talk about sexual abuse to their child:

1. Set some ground rules

Children can comprehend rules faster than adults. Parents can broach the topic of various rules in school and at home, and then add this rule in too, that strangers, or for that matter, no one, is allowed to touch their private parts or take them to lonely places. Even when a child is going to the toilet at school, nobody should be allowed to touch their private part other than the parents when they are cleaning them up. If anything is making the child feel uncomfortable, they must be taught to immediately come and report it to their parents.

2. Communicate to build trust

Make it a habit to ask your child what has happened in school regularly. Ananya Ray, mother of an eight-year-old boy and a friend of mine, told me once, 'I make it a point to discuss everything with my son when he comes back from school. I repeatedly tell him, "We are your parents and we are going to be there for you all the time. You should not hide anything from us." I make it a point that if anything is bothering him, he should discuss it with us. This way, I keep track of what is happening in his life.'

When children grow old enough to understand abuse, parents should sit them down and communicate to them how some people try to get closer to sexually abuse a child. Parents should maintain proper eye contact and not feel shy about talking to them about this matter. Never ignore when a child is asking questions. Answer all their questions, as children are very curious by nature. The more your answer, the greater is the clarity that sets in.

3. Mind the tone

The tone in which you communicate to the child is very important. In this matter, your tone shouldn't be loud, and shouldn't imply that you are warning the child. The tone should indicate sensitivity and it should appear to the child that their parents are building a safety net for them with boundaries, and no one is allowed to cross these boundaries, where physical contact is concerned.

5. Express love, no matter what

Parents need to always remember that children feel it's their fault if they get abused, so they should be made to understand that it is not their fault. If the parent becomes hyper after hearing that something has happened, the child's brain stops processing the event and eventually, the negative conviction surfaces, that it is their fault. The parents should calmly reassure the child and continue telling them that it was not their fault, and they are always there for the child and will always love the child. The child will then feel a sense of safety and reassurance. The brain starts sensing protection.

Importance of touch

Young children thrive on touch; it is one of the most important senses in the early years, and naturally, they show and accept love using this sense the most. Early experiences at touching and being touched are incredibly important—not only for developing later tactile sensitivity, motor skills, and understanding of the physical world but also for health and emotional well-being. If your child associates touch with a traumatic experience, then it will impact their overall development. To keep them away from all kinds of bad touch, keep the following aspects in mind.

- **Avoid violence:** Stop hitting or slapping them, as they start to associate these actions with love. They do not understand what bad touch is, unless explained.

- **Build a vocabulary:** They lack the communication power or vocabulary to share what they experienced with you. Talk to them every night about their day, who they play with, talk to and what kinds of games they indulge in. Keep it simple; do not get anxious.

- **Don't ignore subtle changes:** Many parents think children are imagining this behaviour and thus tend to ignore the child's attempts to talk about it. If your child shares any unusual conversation or shows unusual behaviour, do not ignore it; look into it.

- **Stay calm:** Do not get hyper about it, or your child

will use it as an attention-seeking tactic. Be calm but ensure that you look into all the facts to safeguard your child.

✗ **Use names:** The abuser is usually someone you trust and is confident that you will not suspect them, and that it will be their word against that of a small child. Stop calling everyone an uncle or an aunty.

✗ **Be strict, irrespective of who the abuser is:** The abusers know that most parents are afraid of the social stigma and will thus not take any action against them, and they can move on to the next child. Never be lenient with a child abuser; your child could be at risk again. We have strict laws in our country; demand justice for your child.

Sexual abuse at home

If two children are playing 'Doctor Doctor' or are curious about their genitals, what should you be doing as a parent? Since a young child doesn't yet know the rules of modesty or morality, he's not consciously breaking them when he plays doctor. His curiosity about a playmate's genitals is as natural and as innocent as his curiosity about his own, and motivated more by scientific than sexual interest.

What should the parent do and not do in such a situation?

Punishing, ridiculing, scolding or embarrassing a child for acting on a very natural impulse can confuse, demean, and/or make the activity that's now been 'forbidden', all the more intriguing.

Should a parent tell the child that genitals are bad and so we should not play with them or touch them?

Such a statement by an adult can instil unhealthy feelings about the private parts of the body that can linger through adolescence into adulthood. Such feelings may make the child accept bad things that are done to them by others to their private parts.

If, as a parent, you find your child looking at their genitals or others' genitals, or playing 'Doctor Doctor', what should you do?

It is important to take this opportunity to find out who plays 'Doctor Doctor' with your child and train your child, saying that that there are better games to play, and if anyone wants to play 'Doctor Doctor' with them, then they should say no, and then come and tell you about it.

If you find that another child has kissed your child on the lips, what should you do?

This is a new trend among parents, of kissing their children on their lips. Many find it quite natural, but here is a word of caution against it for two reasons: when you teach your child that kissing on the lips is an acceptable way to show affection, then they will accept it from all adults. Better to teach them then that only their parents can kiss them on the lips.

Stop sharing your bed with your child. When indulging in sexual activity with your spouse, ensure that your child is not around. Even when children are sleeping, they can become aware of it. Many children mimic adult behaviour and might find nothing wrong in doing it with others.

If children ask you about a scene from print or visual media that shows kissing, rape or sexual intimacy, explain to them that is something only adults do when they have mutual consent, and without it, adults can be punished by law. You do not need to talk about this unless your child asks about it. Remember, if children ask about something, it means they are ready to understand it and are curious. It would be better that they get their curiosity satisfied from a known and trusted source rather than a source that can mislead them. Also talk to them about good touch and bad touch, especially when they ask you about rape.

What to do for your child's sexual well-being

1. Ensure that staff appointed by you, like drivers, attendants and watchmen are registered at the nearest police station, or get copies of their Aadhaar card, ration card and driving license.

2. Ask school authorities whether background checks have been done for all teachers and helpers.

3. Teach children about good touch and bad touch in the same manner that you teach them about road safety rhymes. Children are not going to cross the road alone or drive a car, yet we teach them about red light, green light or how to cross at a zebra crossing. In the same way, teach them rhymes about body safety and show them videos on good touch and bad touch.

4. Talk to adults who you know are regularly in touch with your children. Tell them you are concerned about the child's safety and that you have told them to raise an alarm if they feel unsafe. Tell them they should call you in case they know someone who has untoward behaviour.

15

Battling Teenage Depression

It may be hard for parents of teenagers to recognize symptoms and personality traits that indicate depression, as most teens withdraw and try to form their self-identity anyway. I have come across many teens battling masked depression, but most families fail to recognize the symptoms, hence timely help is not given. Unattended depression can predispose young teens to immediate and long-term negative consequences. We all know from experience how adolescence can be one of the loneliest periods of one's life, hence our teens need adequate safety at this age so that they can be healthy young adults with an equally healthy mind.

There are many reasons that can cause teenage depression, and one of them is academic stress. These days, teens are under enormous pressure to succeed academically. Things were not like this when we were children. We don't know if it is good or bad, but as parents also, we cannot ask our children to take it easy, because we need to admit that we live in an inhumanely competitive world where everything is decided on the basis of grades.

During adolescence, after childhood, a child deals with trying to understand a complex world all over again. We need to be cooperative and try to understand that there is a storm inside them, and if we, as parents, don't stand by them, who are they going to ask for support or come back to?

Sometimes, low self-esteem can also lead to this situation, and it is not strange. We, as parents, need to give them the morale boost. As parents, we should not fight with each other in front of our children, because that makes them extremely insecure. Separation can also lead to insecurity among children. And never neglect your child, because emotional neglect can kill their soul. We, as parents, should also be careful while discussing our financial problems.

Parents need to keep reminding themselves that being a teenager is not easy in today's world, where everybody is obsessed about their looks. With the hormonal changes in your child's body, everything changes, and they feel as if Mother Nature is conspiring against them. They cannot accept the way they look, and the way their body has changed. They feel out of place and don't know how to conduct themselves. Parents should be there with their teenage sons/daughters when they are going through such feelings of helplessness.

All these above-mentioned situations can cause mood swings in teenagers which eventually can lead to depression or cause them to turn to alcohol or drugs for a false sense of comfort. Without the necessary coping skills or support, these social stresses can increase the risk of serious depression and, progressively, of suicidal thoughts and behaviour. Genetics also plays a pivotal role in major depressive disorder (MDD).

Sexual feelings are awakened in teenagers because of hormonal and physical changes. Changing hormones cause myriad emotional and behavioural alterations. It has been documented that teenagers provided with sturdy support and guidance cope with these changes better. Usually, between the ages of eight and eighteen years, the body starts growing and changing. These changes occur from head to toe and are completely natural, as the body responds to increased hormone levels. In girls, the main hormone guiding the body's new instructions is called oestrogen, and in boys, it's testosterone. Rewari says that many students who seek help from her as a therapist have learning or attention problems that make it hard for them to succeed in school or college. 'They may feel disappointed in themselves or feel that they are a disappointment to others. Other issues I see are breakups, divorce in the family and academic issues, which, if not attended to, can lead young children into depression.'

Teenagers' brains are still under development, which causes them to be more impulsive, more spontaneous and developmentally not ready to foresee the consequences of their actions. Knowing this can help you better manage your expectations and your relationship with them.

When you see your teenage daughter and son feel sad and down for a period of time that is longer than a couple of weeks, they may be depressed. Depression is an illness, no less real than diabetes or heart disease. It is not the sign of a personal flaw, it is not something you can just snap out of, it is not something to be ashamed of; it is treatable, and everyone has the right to live with a healthy frame of mind.

When your child was young, they believed every word you said. But as a teenager, they are developing their own belief system. It's normal for both of you to disagree sometimes. Instead of arguing over differences in opinion, create an environment where it's safe for both of you to express your ideas.

16

Talking about Periods

Your child should not be clueless about the menstruation cycle, and these days, with girls as young as ten years getting their periods, it is necessary for parents to make their children aware of its significance. When you start seeing your daughter having mood swings and getting irritated for no rhyme or reason, it is time that you sit her down and have a chat with her.[6]

---

[6]Lachmi Deb Roy, 'The period chat with your daughter', *The Times of India*, 20 October 2015, https://timesofindia.indiatimes.com/life-style/relationships/parenting/The-period-chat-with-your-daughter/articleshow/46958396.cms[© Bennett, Coleman & Co. Ltd.]

Here are some ways you can initiate a conversation about periods with your daughter.

Start the chat early

Menstruation is a part of growing up, and there is absolutely no harm if you start the talk early, in small portions. It is quite a scary experience for a child to discover one fine day that she is bleeding. The poor thing may not even know where the blood is coming from. She might think that she is terribly sick or that she is going to die. So, it is important that you begin the chat as soon as you see some changes in your daughter's body, like pubic hair and breast development. She might even ask questions about these slight changes. When you are answering such questions, you can discuss periods as well.

Prepare yourself first

It is important that you prepare yourself first when you start the conversation. Talk about your own experience and be prepared to answer all questions. You might require to go surf the net to study the female reproductive system.

Mental preparation for parents is very important when they sit down for a chat with their children. Make them feel that it is an absolutely normal discussion and maintain eye contact while talking. Since having periods means the onset of sexual maturity, it is important that you inform your daughter about sex and how to be careful about it. There are a lot of questions that might come to a child's mind: How much does bleeding hurt? How often does it happen? Will I be able to play outside with my friends during that time? Clear all doubts that are playing in your daughter's mind. Hold your head high when you have the period chat with your daughter, since you don't want her to feel that it is something that she should be ashamed of.

Avoid bombarding her with too much information

Do not give so much information to the child that they get confused. In fact, the best time to start is when there is a sanitary napkin ad playing on television. Don't give a long lecture about periods in one sitting. Start with small talk, which is easy for your daughter to absorb. Tell her that these are little changes in the body which every girl undergoes, as she gradually becomes a woman. Find out from your daughter's books if they are covering anything about the reproductive system in their school. If they are, it gets easier for you as the mother to explain the topic, as you know that your daughter has some information about it. Don't forget to have an age-appropriate discussion with your daughter.

Basic hygiene

It is important that you teach your child how to use a pad during menstruation and tell her how often she needs to change it. Parents should tell the child about washing her hands thoroughly and to keep her private parts clean so that there is no infection. Teach her the right disposal method.

Common questions that you may have to answer

- ✖ Why do only girls get periods?
- ✖ Does it hurt?
- ✖ How long does it last?
- ✖ Can I play during this time?

Ways to deal with PMS

Premenstrual syndrome (PMS) can be severe for some girls.

1. She must have at least three servings of calcium-rich food a day, such as low-fat milk, cheese, yogurt, fortified orange juice and soya milk.
2. Don't stop her from being physically active. Help her maintain a healthy body weight.
3. Make sure she avoids processed food.
4. Increase her water intake.
5. She should avoid junk food.[7]

---

[7]Lachmi Deb Roy, 'The period chat with your daughter', *The Times of India*, 20 October 2015, https://timesofindia.indiatimes.com/lifestyle/relationships/parenting/The-period-chat-with-your-daughter/articleshow/46958396.cms[© Bennett, Coleman & Co. Ltd.]

17

Preparing for a Younger Sibling

While you and your partner will no doubt be excited to extend the family, it can be a difficult time for your elder child. Having a second child can be an overwhelming experience for both the parents, but it can affect the first child psychologically. There will be innumerable changes in the family life, and the attention that you used to give to your elder one will get divided. Therefore, it is important to prepare your first child for a sibling and help them be a part of the process.

Break the news appropriately

The moment the elder child notices the mother's growing belly, there will be a lot of questions. The preparation should start early. There may be a lot of questions that will come to a child's mind, like where babies come from, and how babies are 'made'? As mothers, we need to explain it to them in a language that they understand, and is appropriate for their age. Tell them that there is a baby canal from which the baby comes out and it takes time for the baby to form inside the mother's tummy.

Correct timing plays a very important role. It is best when you tell the child once you yourself get to know that you are carrying. This will give them some time to process and understand what is happening.

Get your child involved

Making them an important part of the process from the very beginning helps in strengthening the bond. Once in a while, you can take your elder child with you when you go for your check-ups. Taking their opinions in making choices for the newborn, like buying a dress or a rattle will greatly help in building a positive bond. From the very beginning, by showing photographs and videos of the child's infancy, make them understand that their mother will have to carry the newborn around the way she had done it for them.

A lot depends on the age gap between the first and second child. If the gap is of two to three years, then it is not going to be easy because at this stage, parents mean the world to kids. Make your child touch your stomach and feel the bulge. This will help them understand better. Talk to them about the positives of having a sibling and how it is important for them to have company.

Spend time with them

It is equally important for both the parents to spend adequate time with the child during the last few weeks of pregnancy, as it will make them feel important. Make sure your first child knows that they are an important part of the family, and make them understand how important their contributions are to the family. Make your child feel special by telling them that without their help, things will not go smoothly. The father should slowly get involved in spending more time with the elder child. Fathers should cultivate a fun relationship with their elder child.

As the day scheduled for the delivery arrives, spend as much time with them as possible.

Dealing with jealousy

It is natural for the elder child to feel a little insecure. No matter how much time you give them during your pregnancy, and even after the baby arrives, there will be times when they will crave more. Deal with it patiently and allow your elder child to express their feelings. When the newborn arrives, encourage the older child to talk about their feelings about the baby. Do not expect the child to share everything at the first go. Give them time.

Jealousy is actually an emotion the child does not understand. They have been the centre of the universe for so long, that the entry of another entity who howls and needs constant attention can be disturbing. To add to that, everyone who comes to visit is in awe of this new creature, and the older child may get upset at the division of attention.

Talking to the child calmly, paying attention and having someone look after the baby for a while so that you can focus on the older one does help in dealing with the situation.

Encouraging a connection

The older the child, the better you can explain and introduce the concept of another child joining your family to them. When the elder child is just two or three years old, they are not independent and need help too, and parents mean the world to them. If the gap is of six or seven years, it is a lot easier for the elder child to cope, as they have their own circle of friends and fixed play and school time. To develop a bond, parents should let the elder one feel responsible by allowing them to hold the baby when they are around and involving the child in small chores like getting the milk bottle, and then appreciating them for all the little things that they do. Involving the older child in preparing the home for a new baby, buying baby stuff, checking out their old baby clothes to see what you can reuse, getting the stroller and bed fitted and putting together a few safe toys are practical ways to begin.

Tell your firstborn that they are your baby and the newborn would be *their* baby. They will take this very seriously and try to behave in a very responsible and almost motherly or fatherly manner when the newborn arrives. Teach them how to fold diapers, tell them to help you out in cleaning and changing the younger one. Teach them to read out stories and sing a song for the younger one. Each parent can see what works for them. Grandparents too need to spend time with the older child and not ignore the elder one over the newborn.

18

Mean Children Need to Be Heard

If you want to curb the 'mean girl' attitude in teen girls, such as Lindsay Lohan portrayed in the 2004 film of the same name, try intervention. Mean girls more often than not have mean parents! Meanness is a learnt behaviour. A child learns this kind of behaviour through observation of how people behave at home, and in other places where they spend time. So, if a child is left at their grandparents' home or at their home and sees their grandparents and parents behaving nastily with the house help, neighbours, etc., then they get used to ascertaining that this is 'normal'.[8]

This is a story I did for *The Times of India* a couple of years back. For writing this chapter too, I spoke to a couple of psychologists to understand how to deal with mean children. Here is how you can prevent your teenage girl from being a mean LiLo girl.[9]

1. Set a good example in front of your teenage girl

It's very important for mothers to know that young teen girls consciously and subconsciously emulate them. Mothers are the first role models for teens; the way you dress up, your gestures and behaviour patterns are all slowly imprinted on your teen girl. To impart healthy behaviour, it's important that mothers themselves should be kind and compassionate towards family, friends and their spouse. Become an example for your child. Parents, especially mothers, influence girls more than they can imagine. So, if you are the perfect role model for her and you set good examples in front of her,

---

[8]Lachmi Deb Roy, 'Is your teen the mean "LiLo" girl?' *The Times of India*, 8 June 2015, https://timesofindia.indiatimes.com/life-style/relationships/parenting/Is-you-teen-the-mean-Lilo-girl/articleshow/46985308.cms[© Bennett, Coleman & Co. Ltd.]
[9]ibid

then that's the best way to prevent meanness in your child.

2. Point it out to her that being mean has never helped anybody

Point out examples of how mean people are usually, over time, alienated by society. That by being mean, she will slowly start losing friends and become lonely. Tell her that she might get short-term pleasures by being mean. Make her realize that the long-term consequences of her actions will not be good.

Never vent your family frustrations or your job frustration or rather any kind of frustration in front of your teenager.

The root cause of being mean and selfish is also when your teen girl is harbouring resentment and hostility in her mind for the harm she feels is done to you. She will not comprehend that your emotional display was temporary. This is the starting point of being mean, and it slowly gets woven into the fabric of one's personality. As parents, we need to be very careful as to when we are narrating a mean act or are on an emotional drive about our in-laws, friends or any other family members.

3. Make your teenage daughter confident

Meanness is often a result of jealousy, and jealousy is often a result of low self-worth. If you feel that your child suffers from meanness, then look for signs of inferiority in them. If they are insecure and suffer from an inferiority complex, then help your child develop self-assurance. That is the crux.

4. Be positive with your teens

The basic language of love you use with your teen should be full of positive and warm statements. The more you appreciate and express love, the more she extends this warmth outside her family domain. Do you know that teens are the reflections of their parents? One way to make your teen learn new patterns is to establish daily sharing, or exchange of kind words. This will make sure the rudeness and meanness are at bay.

5. Be an active listener

As your teen grows older and develops new interests and friends, she seeks validation. This desire needs to be fulfilled at home. Then she develops into a secure teenager. Secure children are always happy and non-judgemental. They are always kind and compassionate beings. Always listen to what your teenage girl has to say, maintain eye contact and be focused. The more she feels loved and accepted, the more the negative feelings will dissipate.

6. Correct her when she is mean

When your teen is stepping out of the boundaries and starts becoming mean to other relatives or friends, it's the mother's fundamental duty to make sure that this behaviour is checked and then stopped altogether. Communicate with your teen girl and tell her the consequences of being a mean child. Do so with adequate reasoning and calmness. Just dismissing the teen and telling her she is a bad girl might exacerbate the problem. Teens are like malleable clay; moulding largely depends on how gently we handle it. It's a learning process for both the parents and the young teenage daughter. Even if you falter a first, keep trying.

How to spot the signs of a mean girl[10]

1. **She is always envious:** She is always competing with friends, sisters and cousins for everything, be it clothes, grades or boyfriends. She can go to any extreme to get things she desires and always gets things done her way.

2. **She doesn't appreciate anybody:** She refuses to acknowledge the good qualities of others.

3. **She is very dominating:** She always wants to control everything, be it a relationship or any plans. She loves to take charge of others. She wants everybody to follow her.

4. **She is more like a frenemy:** A mean girl is more of a frenemy than a friend. She loves to back-bite about others and gossip.

5. **She is overtly competitive:** She is very ambitious and overly competitive about the way she looks and presents herself. She thinks she is the best and can go to the extent

---

[10]Lachmi Deb Roy, 'Is your teen the mean "LiLo" girl?' *The Times of India*, 8 June 2015, https://timesofindia.indiatimes.com/life-style/relationships/parenting/Is-you-teen-the-mean-Lilo-girl/articleshow/46985308.cms[© Bennett, Coleman & Co. Ltd.]

of back-stabbing and dirty politics to achieve what she wants.

Dealing with bad habits in children

Some children are seen to throw tantrums, especially when they want something and the parents refuse to give in to it. But sometimes, this tantrum can turn out to be a nightmare. What parents can do about this is walk away from it. Ignoring is the best thing. Paying a lot of attention to bad habits or pushing your child away may actually have a negative impact on the child. If you give them too much attention, chances are that they will be sitting on your head and will be encouraged to repeat the behaviour.

When the child shows good behaviour and discipline, it is good to praise and reward them. Let them know that you were happy as parents with their good habits to give them a morale boost to behave well throughout their life. This will help them develop a sense of trust towards their parents. We, as parents, need to make a conscious effort to educate our children about good and bad behaviour and also make them understand how bad behaviour is unhealthy for their own personal development.

Many children have the habit of picking fights. Aggression in children is not a good sign. They generally pick fights in playgrounds or in school when parents are not around. Aggressive children are those who are always craving attention. It is important for parents to figure out the cause of aggression when they get complaints from the school or some other parent. Do not overreact and start hitting your child. Sit with your child and analyse the situation. If your child is watching violent movies or cartoons, it is time to intervene. Engage them in some useful activity which helps them to vent their emotions.

Some children pick up the habit of showing disrespect to elders. Behaving badly with grandparents and house helps is not a good sign. Children generally pick up these habits from those around them, especially parents and elder siblings. Set good examples for them and be polite to everyone around them. They will pick up the good habits of greeting and thanking from parents. When you are talking to your house help, be careful about the words you use and the way you behave, because remember, your children are constantly watching and observing what you are doing.

Talking back is another bad behaviour that needs to be corrected at the earliest. Children become argumentative as they grow older, and once they are in their teens, they start developing a mind of their own. Talking back gradually becomes a habit. Parents should take up the matter early in their child's life because, as children grow older, it gets difficult for parents to deal with this bad habit and for children to correct old habits.

19

Ready for Adoption?

re you considering adopting a second child? There are certain questions you should ask yourself before taking the plunge for adopting a second child in spite of having a biological child. Remember, every adoption is unique. Adoption requires lifelong commitment, and adopting a second child becomes a little bit trickier when you already have a biological child.

One needs to be honest with oneself. Sometimes, parents adopt to give a sibling to the first child because a single child is a lonely child. But there are a lot of medical reasons for which they may not be in a condition to have a second child. For some, the desire of giving company to the first child comes much later in life. Sometimes, doctors say that having a child in your forties is not safe. So, adoption becomes the best option. There are others who want to give a good life to a child and hence go for adoption. Whatever the reason, such decisions should not be taken in haste and one should keep the practical perspective in mind.

Are you ready for the hard work it takes to adopt?

Adopting can get very daunting, as there is a lot of paperwork involved in it. One needs to be logical and cool-headed till it goes through. To get the adopted child used to the new environment, sometimes mothers need to take a sabbatical or pick up a part-time job. She should be mentally prepared for this change in her life. As a parent, one needs to give the adopted child a lot more time to understand their temperament. As parents, one should prepare oneself for celebrating the differences and should not draw any comparison with the biological child.

What should be the best age group for adoption?

It is always better to adopt an infant because if you are adopting a child who is three or four years old, then the initial formative years are gone. If you adopt an infant then it becomes easy for the parents to connect with the child. The child then can automatically adapt to the set pattern of living, behaving and eating.

How is the parenting of an adopted child different from that of a biological child?

A biological child is a part of one's body and is already bonded with in the womb of the mother. Seema Hingorrany says, 'There are some habits which are genetic and cannot be avoided. Many traits travel through genes. Parents need to be patient. One needs to be intelligent enough to understand how to deal with this situation. Sometimes the adopted child may require professional counselling, and as parents they should not shy away from it.' Many a time, adopted children can suffer from attention deficit hyperactivity disorder (ADHD) which happens due to nutrition deficiency when the child is in the mother's womb. Such situations should be handled clinically.

I spoke to a friend who had adopted a child and she had to say that her adopted child had a habit of flicking things. My friend was extremely depressed when she discovered this. The child used to pick up cutlery from restaurants. It used to get very embarrassing and sometimes it became difficult to keep track of what she was doing. There used to be complaints coming from school as well, and it got terribly upsetting for the parents. But then they took the help of a child counsellor and started spending a lot of time with her. And finally they are happy that she has come out of the habit of flicking.

Is it important to disclose to your adopted child that they are not your biological child?

It is a good idea to disclose to your second child that they are adopted. And it is always better that they get to know from the parents and not anybody else. But that should be at a proper age and you should give them the assurance that you love them equally, and make the child feel secure. Be prepared to answer all of your child's queries about their parents, background and the reasons behind their adoption. The adopted child may go to the extent of wanting to meet their birth mother. It is important that you prepare yourself and handle such situations tactfully.

Why is it important to discuss it with your elder child?

Adopting a second child is a major decision and it is important that parents discuss this topic with the first child before taking the decision. It is as important as discussing it with your spouse because sometimes they have to be prepared for this change. It should be a collective decision if you do not want your family life to suffer. The more the biological child is prepared, the better they will be to adapt to this change. Give some time to your biological child to think about it and then take a call. Involving them in the adoption of your second child can make them feel included in the process. Prepare your biological child for all the questions that relatives and friends may ask them. A heart to heart is important in such situations.

How should we share the news with family and friends, especially grandparents?

Firstly, no matter how open-minded one's family is, one should be prepared for some lukewarm responses, and some cold ones too. My advice is that if you, your spouse and your biological child have decided on taking the plunge of adopting a child, relatives and friends should just be informed, and parents should be firm with their decisions and not get carried away by what relatives say. But at the same time, you should bring the grandparents into confidence and answer all their questions without getting annoyed. As your adopted child grows up, prepare them mentally that there may be discrimination from others at many points in their life, but for parents, both the children are equally precious.

20

Three Is Company

Whether it is the rising monetary concerns, late first-time pregnancy, career-oriented couples or the anxiety of going through labour pain all over again, a single-child family is slowly becoming a norm in most urban homes. Many of my friends mentioned that since they got married in their thirties, they decided on having a single child.

With the exceedingly expensive life we lead today, starting a family can be challenging by itself. Having a single child has become more of a compulsion than a choice for many. For those who have a choice, a single child can be both an advantage and a disadvantage. If you're parents of a single child and contemplating a second one, here's looking at the pros and cons of raising a single child that you can base your decision on.[11]

Single child, double the love

Having a single child means you can give undivided time and love to your child. At the same time, raising a single child becomes more economical, as parents do not need to compromise on their aspirations for their child, and can provide the best of everything to them. Looking at the escalating expenses of schools and extra-curricular classes, having a single child helps financially. Also, parents who don't have much patience and a low threshold of endurance can handle things and crises better with one child, as the

---

[11]Lachmi Deb Roy, 'How to raise a happy single child', *The Times of India*, 13 March 2015, https://timesofindia.indiatimes.com/life-style/relationships/parenting/How-to-raise-a-happy-single-child/articleshow/44210377.cms[© Bennett, Coleman & Co. Ltd.]

level of frustration is lower with less responsibility.

Raising confident single children[12]

In many cases, when a child has a sibling, they may suffer from the negative impact of sibling rivalry, leading to insecurity or competition. As a result, with a single child, there are higher chances of the child turning out to be confident and self-sufficient. This, in turn, results in them being better achievers and extroverts with adequate social skills, quite suited to this age's cut-throat competitive world.

No sibling, no sharing

With all the love showered upon a single child, they might be very possessive about their belongings as well as relationships. Due to the undivided attention that a single child gets, there is a high possibility that they might take

---

[12]Lachmi Deb Roy, 'How to raise a happy single child', *The Times of India*, 13 March 2015, https://timesofindia.indiatimes.com/lifestyle/relationships/parenting/How-to-raise-a-happy-single-child/articleshow/44210377.cms[© Bennett, Coleman & Co. Ltd.]

more time to learn the fundamental aspects of sharing and giving. Parents have to make extra effort to spend more time with the child, as the child usually has no one to share their feelings with and express their emotions to, till they learn to do that with friends later.

It can get lonely sometimes

One of the main reasons parents opt for a second pregnancy is to ensure that their child doesn't get lonely, and has someone to support and care for them throughout their life. However, parents with a single child are finding alternative ways to ensure that their children enjoy the same amount of interaction as they would have with their siblings. What I personally do is I expand my circle of friends and try and maintain a good relationship with them and sometimes go the extra mile to keep in touch with friends and relatives. Since his childhood days, my child has grown up amidst company, as we plan our holidays together, and he has my friends' kids to play with. As a result, he has learnt to make friends and has a big circle of friends. They spend time in each others' houses during weekends and play together in the evenings.

Things to remember when raising a single child

1. Encourage more interactions within the family and outside, by inviting play dates, so that the child can enhance their social skills.

2. Though they are your only child, don't spoil them by giving in to all their demands. Set your expectations and ensure that your child understands the consequences of irresponsible actions.

3. Allow your child to express their feelings about others having a sibling and the fact that they don't.

4. Once your child is of a suitable age, provide an explanation about your choice of having only one child, and assure them that it is in their best interest.

5. From the time they turn two, teach your child concepts of sharing and giving through stories, games, etc.

6. Spend as much time as you can with your child to make sure that they are not lonely.

7. Bring home a pet if your child feels very lonely, as pets provide companionship and often fill in the role of a virtual sibling.

21

Dealing with a Child's Sexual Orientation

It takes a lot of courage for kids to come up to their parents and discuss their sexual orientation. It takes time for parents to accept things they don't understand, but we should remember that it has got nothing to do with their upbringing. If your child is not straight, then it is not his, or your, fault. We just need to learn to accept and should be willing to listen to him.

Mamma, I am gay[13]

Disclosing your sexual preference to your parents is not easy, but parents can allow their child to express themselves by not judging their feelings.

A twenty-six-year-old boy, Rohan, had to call off his engagement with his fiancé, because he couldn't keep pretending that he was straight. He could not muster the courage to refuse the proposal initially, as he was scared of his parents' reaction. But when he could not take the pressure any more, he told his parents that he was gay and had a boyfriend. It is difficult for most parents to accept the fact that their child is gay. However, it is also tough for the youngster, who not only has to cope with his repressed feelings but also the backlash at the disclosure. So, when is the right time for a person to come out to his family?

---

[13]Lachmi Deb Roy, 'Mamma, I'm gay,' *The Times of India*, 13 February 2015, https://timesofindia.indiatimes.com/life-style/relationships/love-sex/Mamma-Im-gay/articleshow/42452367.cms

Broaching the topic

The right time for every individual is different, and it depends on the comfort level he shares with his family. It is also important for him to know that it's not just a phase. Coming to terms with one's sexual orientation differs from age to age. It is different for younger age groups as they undergo huge guilt and confusion towards their orientation. Financial independence can allow a certain level of fearlessness about expressing feelings. For those dependent on their parents, coming out of the closet, they fear, would cause their parents to disown them.

Lakshmi Narayan Tripathy, Chairperson, Astitva, and founding member of Asia Pacific Transgender Network, told me when I was conducting research on the topic, 'Sexually different children are often confused about who they are, and the biggest irony is, people around us decide who we are. The education system needs to change too. I have seen boys who are different getting abused in schools, and these cases do not even get reported. They should have trained counsellors in schools.'[14]

---

[14]Lachmi Deb Roy, 'How to raise a happy single child', *The Times*

Financial independence is very important so that you can come out and speak for yourself and lead your life according to your own terms. So, building up a career is very important before you open up.

Different parents, different reactions

For most Indians, a relationship between a man and a woman is the only normal one and same-sex orientation is perceived as a Western concept. Even when we try to be open-minded about it, we are not able to accept it completely. It may come as a shock for parents who don't have any idea about their child's orientation. There are some parents who, in spite of knowing about it, are in a state of denial.

No matter how modern parents are in India today, either they do not believe in or are in total denial about their children's sexual orientation. Parents cannot accept the fact that their child will have a same-sex partner as high hopes are built to carry the family name forward

---

of India, 13 March 2015, https://timesofindia.indiatimes.com/life-style/relationships/parenting/How-to-raise-a-happy-single-child/articleshow/44210377.cms[© Bennett, Coleman & Co. Ltd.]

by marrying and procreating. They cry, sob, blame God and run to palmists and spiritual leaders in a state of helplessness. Psychologist Seema Hingorrany told me in an interview, 'Many come to us to do a family therapy session, to help their family cope with emotions following disclosure. At times, parents may experience a sense of loss akin to death. Though it does take time, there are many who accept it and stand by their children. A parent with a gay son told me during an interview, "It did take some time for me to understand. There were many unanswered questions that kept playing in my mind, but then I finally accepted the fact that my son is gay, and not a criminal. He has not harmed anybody and has every right to lead his life peacefully."'[15]

Questions parents need to ask their children

1. Do you identify with your assumed sexual orientation?
2. Do you have a good support system?

---

[15]Lachmi Deb Roy, 'How to raise a happy single child', *The Times of India*, 13 March 2015, https://timesofindia.indiatimes.com/life-style/relationships/parenting/How-to-raise-a-happy-single-child/articleshow/44210377.cms[© Bennett, Coleman & Co. Ltd.]

3. What is your current emotional situation?
4. Are you usually a patient person?
5. What is your reason for coming out now?

22

Is Your Child Happy?

Being a parent is one of the most difficult yet rewarding jobs on the planet. Being responsible for another person may seem scary or overwhelming and may result in you overparenting your child. You can avoid this by helping your child become mature, giving them some independence, helping them solve problems, and dealing with your own worries. As parents, we should guide them in the right direction, respect their views as well and never overshadow them.

Sometimes, when our children are unhappy, we tend to overreact and try to make them feel okay. If they are uncertain about their future, we may mistake this for deep insecurity and shower them with praise and assurance. We always get worried if we sense the slightest discomfort in our children, and negative thoughts pour into our heads. We keep questioning ourselves and we bog them down with more questions, and even if they are not worried, they tend to get irritated.

If our children are unhappy, we tend to overreact and try our best to lift their spirits. If your child is unhappy, sit down and explain to them that everything doesn't happen the way they want. Give your child time, and that is for sure going to help them. But give them some free time to think about their life as well. You will not be able to do any good to them if you try to bubble-wrap them from all hurdles of life. Let them feel the scorching heat of the sun, let them cross rocky paths and let them feel the thorns under their feet, because that is the way they are going to learn. We don't want to mess up our child's happiness, but we shouldn't mollycoddle them all the time, because that is the surest way of messing up their life.

We all want the same things for our children. We want them to grow up to love and be loved, to follow their dreams, to find success. Mostly, though, we want them to be happy. But just how much control do we have over our children's happiness?

Ask any parent what they want for their child, and the unanimous answer would be 'Happiness!' However, that's one state that cannot be controlled. A recent research by psychologists at the University of Edinburgh and the Queensland Institute for Medical Research in Australia states that happiness can be inherited, which means that parents have a hand in ensuring the child grows up to be a happy child.[16] Here are some simple things that they should keep in mind while raising their children into happy and contented adults:

1. Happy children

Happy children are a product of happy homes. Your state of mind, depression or happiness makes an impact on the child

---

[16]Live Science Staff, 'Happiness Is Partly Inherited,' *Live Science*, 3 March 2008, https://www.livescience.com/2346-happiness-partly-inherited.html

during conception. When couples are happy, the possibility of conception is high. A woman should always try to keep herself in a good mood during pregnancy, as a happy state of mind makes happy children.

2. Stay connected

For your child's lifelong emotional well-being, it is important that there is a close bond in the family. In fact, they should be taught to connect with all the members in the house, including grandparents, cousins, friends, neighbours, domestic helps and pets. Spend as much time as possible with your children and give them unconditional love. Hug your children, hold them and appreciate them for their achievements. Encourage them to socialize. The more connections your child makes, the better it is for their development.

4. Happy parents raise happy children

It is important for parents to have a healthy, understanding relationship between themselves because it affects the psyche of their children. It is not just about a parent's relationship with the child. It is also about how happy the mother and the father are together as a couple. The responsibility of parenting should be shared so that nobody feels the pressure.

Small gestures count

I try to remember all the time what is it that made us feel loved as children. For me, it was always about having a great time with my mother, since I had a very detached father. Probably that was his style of parenting. Sometimes it was about holidays, sharing a few fun secrets and also sharing your dreams. As parents, are we doing enough to make our children feel loved? Very often, it is the little gestures that count. One just needs to put in that little effort and time.

1. **Switch off distractions:** Turn off your smartphones or just keep them away from you. When you get home after a long day at work or if you are a stay-at-home mom, when your children return from school, just give them a tight hug and talk to them about how their day was. Discuss your day too. Make it a fun conversation. You don't need to fiddle with your mobile. You just need to sit and be with them. Don't answer any messages post

eight o'clock in the night.

2. **Dinner time, fun time:** Make dinner time a fun event in the house, where both the parents and the children participate and talk about life in general, the happenings around the world, friends and more. Turn off all gadgets and don't keep texting during meal times. You can even talk about food and the dish that they enjoy eating the most, and why it is important to relish food, the importance of nutrition and a balanced diet. Tell them why food wastage should be made a criminal offence— because there are so many children around us who don't even get a single morsel of food to eat every day.

3. **Show physical affection:** Hug your child often. If you want a happy child, always remember that children thrive on love and affection. If a child is loved, they feel wanted, and this helps in developing their self-esteem. You must have observed that children who come from happy families do not suffer from behavioural problems. They are much more secure, as they feel their family is always with them. If you have a young child who is not yet a teenager, shower them with loads of hugs and kisses. But if you feel your teenage daughter or son

is getting embarrassed with your hugging and kissing gestures, change your gestures. Be generous with your teenagers with your praises, appreciation and use an affectionate tone when you are talking to them.

4. **Bedtime should be precious**: With young children, make bedtime a precious moment. Remember, as your children grow older and step into teenage followed by adulthood, it is these moments that they are going to cherish throughout their life. Read them a story from a book, or just cook it up yourself. It is a beautiful feeling to see them drift off into sleep, and it is a unique bonding experience both for children and parents. Storytelling during bedtime, or maybe anytime, helps them develop their imagination skills.

5. **Treat all children equally**: Spend quality time with each of your children. Remember, children feel special and open up better when there is nobody about except the two of you. You can involve them in any kind of activity, like playing a game of tennis, or reading a book together or just talking to each other. It is during these times that you discover a lot about your child. If you have two children, divide the time equally between

them. Do not neglect one child for the other. They, at any cost, should not feel that their mother is being partial and loves one child more than the other. Even if there are some grievances or complaints, they will be able to open up better to you that way.

6. **Be a role model**: Be careful how you speak to others in front of them and mind your language always. Be polite, and no matter how worked-up or tired you are, remember your child is watching your actions. So don't throw tantrums or be rude to your house helps. Children always knowingly or unknowingly try to ape their parents. When it comes to parenting, I have seen many parents being overtly competitive. Don't be competitive; teach your child to just follow their heart and compete with themselves, and not others.

7. **Involve your child in decision-making**: It is also important to respect their decisions. Don't just impose your views on them. Ask them their opinion—what they feel about a certain thing. It can be as simple as dressing up for a party. Ask them what colour they wish to wear and if you wish to go colour-coordinated as a family, then also you should ask them about their choice of

colour. Sometimes they want their mothers and fathers to dress up in a certain way; sometimes you can keep their wish too, until and unless their expectations are completely bizarre.

8. **Be spontaneous:** Play with them as much as you can—these can be unorganized games too. Don't make them schedule slaves. Children love to spend some unstructured time with their parents, when they can just laugh and play and relax.

9. **Address their worries:** Be there for your child when you feel something is bothering them, or they are unhappy. There may be someone in school or hobby class, and sometimes even a teacher who is bullying them. Try and take charge of the situation by spending time with them. Show them that you care, and try and find out their cause of unhappiness and put them at ease. Most importantly, try and find out the cause of your child's stress and who the people involved in it are. Teach them life skills on how to deal with bullies.

10. **Treasure their gifts:** Children have beautiful ways of showing affection. Sometimes they make cards or write poems for their parents. You, as parents, in turn should

show your happiness and treasure those gifts by hanging them on the soft board of your bedroom, attaching it with a magnet on the fridge. These actions of yours give a great sense of achievement to the children.

11. **Don't interrupt:** When your child has a story to tell, just listen to them carefully. Don't interrupt them. The story can be a simple school event or an incident at the park or maybe a discussion with a friend. No matter how busy you are, never ignore them. If you do, chances are, they will never share any of the stories of their life with you. Always encourage your children to speak their heart out and make sure you listen to them carefully. Love and affection are the foundations of a happy child.

23

True Meaning of Success

We should help children define success in a positive way. But first, we should ask ourselves certain questions.

1. Am I aware of my child's academic strengths and weaknesses?
2. What are the other activities my child is fond of other than studies?
3. Am I thrusting my own interests on my child?

Once we, as parents, are clear about these issues and find answers to these questions, half the battle is won. We all want success and we want our children to be successful too. But have you ever asked yourself what success actually is? To understand success, we need to know what success is not. We all want to be successful and feel successful. We chase money, power, fame and what not, and at the end of the day, we end up being disappointed and unhappy. Why? Because we didn't know where to stop. This is exactly what we need to tell children…STOP and THINK when you feel you are pushing too hard.

We, as parents, need to teach our children to learn from their mistakes and also the mistakes we have made as a child. We need to ensure that they don't repeat them. Tell them that those who have achieved the greatest success in life are those who are crystal clear in their mind and know exactly what it means to reach the top. So, if we want our children to be successful, the first and most important thing to instil in them is clarity of mind.

Then we need to teach our children what success isn't. Tell them that success is not only about making wealth, making an impressive CV and having a huge social media following. It is more than that. Tell them that even if the entire world thinks that they are not good enough, they should give their whole heart and soul into whatever interests them, and when they achieve success in that, they feel that nothing could have been better than that. And once they know that they have put in their full effort and what they have achieved is the ultimate, they have a taste of success. But again, that shouldn't be the end of the journey; in fact, it should be the beginning.

It is okay if our children idolize somebody, but we shouldn't teach them to be like somebody else. Teach them that it is okay to fall, but what is important is how you get up after the fall with your head held high. Winston Churchill rightly said, 'Success is not final, failure is not fatal. It is the courage to continue that counts.'

When we compliment our child, we shouldn't say something like 'You are going to be the next Obama', if they are good at oratory, or 'You are going to be the next Picasso or M.F. Husain' if they are good at painting. Let them be the first one. Being like somebody is not going to make our children successful. There are many people who have climbed the ladder of success to find that it is extremely lonely at the top, and they do feel miserable and burned out. Teach them to give their best and also, at the same time, teach them to balance life in a proper and mature manner. Let them know that not all successful people are happy.

How to balance both work life and personal life is a very important lesson we must teach our children, so that they grow up to be happy adults. Teach them that success is not about wealth and power only; it is much more than that. Different people have different ideas of success which they form from their parents, teachers, siblings or friends. Although it is okay to value the opinion of others, at the end of the day, we must teach our children that everything boils down to them and their happiness. It is good to keep your parents and elders happy, but first the child needs to be happy. One cannot pour from an empty cup; if we are drained out trying to keep up with everybody's demands, how are we going to spread happiness?

Some people think success means attaining a certain object. Success according to the norms of the world is not the end of everything. We should make our children understand that success means inner happiness and that nothing is more important than that. It is not about obtaining a specific object, a high-paying job or a social status. Sometimes success can be the result of the greatest failure!

Success differs from person to person. Some people feel that helping others or following their passion brings them the greatest joy. So everybody has a different way of looking at success. The simplest truth of life is that what makes one happy cannot make others happy too. It is important for parents to find out what makes their children happy. If your child is fond of the subject English and wants to pursue English Literature when they grow up, it is important for you to respect your child's desires and not force them to take up Medicine or Engineering just because you want them to study those subjects. It is good to be their guiding light, but never ever impose your views on them such that they forget themselves.

24

Don't Forget to Take Care of Yourself

We, as parents, too need to take care of ourselves and our own happiness, and we shouldn't get bogged down by parenthood. Mothers, especially, in the mad chase of taking care of children, and the family, forget to take care of themselves. This is a lesson that I had learnt a few years back and I don't want anybody else to learn it the way I did. I still recall the date, 28 November 2014. I came back from office with a mild headache and thought it was normal, and as usual popped a painkiller so that I could finish my household chores. With my husband away for work and my single parenting, with my eight-year-old son in a city that I had moved to after nearly a decade, it wasn't easy. Soon, I could feel the thumping headache and my whole body started aching. I had low-grade fever too. I remember popping another painkiller, thinking it was the flu affecting me because of regular exertion. I had promised my son that we would go out for dinner. But I lay on the bed, and turning from one side to another became a pain. The pain was such that a truck had run over me.

When my son saw me feeling so drained out, he sensed the seriousness of my illness and called my mother. Every inch of my body was hurting. I couldn't move. I was taken to the hospital and all the tests of dengue and malaria were done. The moment the needle pricked my left arm, it flared up. I had absolutely no clue as to what was happening to me. There were blisters all over my left arm. Somehow, I managed to reach home. My speech was disrupted. I was feeling completely disoriented. I still remember a few junior doctors asking me whether I had taken some kind of drugs or alcohol. I kept on saying, 'I don't even take aerated drinks, and I count each calorie that goes into my system.'

Moving from one place to another became a task. I used to literally drag myself to the washroom. I did not feel like eating anything. My entire mouth was red and my throat was burning. I felt nauseous all the time. I was throwing up whatever I was eating. My left big toe and right foot started swelling up. Initially, the doctor thought the swelling on my toe to be gout. But my uric acid count was normal. Then what was it? I became completely immobile. My condition started deteriorating at a terrifying pace. Realizing that it was something serious, I called the ambulance and got myself admitted to the hospital. My neighbour accompanied me. I was diagnosed with sepsis.

A quick check-up by the nephrologist at the hospital made her realize that I didn't have much time left. I was immediately rushed to the ICU where I was diagnosed with severe sepsis. Lying on the hospital bed, I could literally feel death calling me. I was scared of shutting my eyes because I didn't want to pass away in my sleep. In my dazed state, I was constantly pleading to God to give me just ten more years so that I could see my son become independent, and it would be easy for me to shut my eyes in peace. Though everything was blurry, at the back of my mind I knew I had responsibilities to fulfil. I couldn't believe how my life changed in a matter of a few days. Till my illness, nobody in my family had heard of sepsis. My husband was called back from sea by the naval fraternity because my condition started deteriorating rapidly.

By then, the disease had immobilized me completely. But I fought really hard. All my organs were shutting down. Moving around in a stretcher was also painful. My left hand was rotting. The worst thing happened when I realized that I was forgetting things. I was in a semi-comatose state where I could feel everything happening around me yet couldn't react to it. Despite the severe pain, I was ready to fight.

Every day I was struggling to live. Though I had very little chance of survival, I defied the odds. It was my little son who kept me going. I wanted to live for him. When I started getting a little better, the only thing I kept asking the battalion of doctors was when I could go back home to see my son getting ready for school and going to the park to play.

Recovering from sepsis was an extremely slow process. It took me nearly a year to recover. Since I had lost strength completely and my feet were swollen, taking each step was a pain. Doctors had doubts about whether I would be able to walk again. They were suspecting that the damage was permanent. My doctors told me clearly that I had to rethink everything that I had done in life, hinting at giving up my career in journalism. But I was in a fight with my life. Initially, I started walking with the help of a walker and an attendant used to be by my side to help me. It was like learning how to walk all over again. I practised walking as much as I could.

I still remember the day when I was able take a few steps without the help of my walker. Seeing me walk without any help, my mother started clapping her hands with tears in her eyes. Though I was limping, I remember my son said to lift up my spirits, 'Mom, you are walking just like the way you used to before; I am sure you will be able to climb the stairs soon.' My friends who came to visit me in the ICU had to say that they were unable to recognize me because I had lost weight drastically and my skin had started peeling off.

I did go back to work after a leave of two months. But I could continue only for a few months, as my health was giving up again. I took a sabbatical from journalism for a year. Again, staying at home made me feel depressed. So, I started teaching Media Studies to postgraduate students.

Work helped me cope with my health better. Slowly I learnt how to climb steps, though for a very long time I walked with a limp. I started practising yoga. I just gave myself time. Today I participate in any marathon that takes place in the city. I don't compete with anybody, but myself. One thing that I have learnt is to not take on stress, because I feel it is really not worth it.

I fought really hard, and I consider myself to be lucky to be alive and thriving. I regularly run marathons, but I know how well I ran for my life. There are so many people who die of sepsis without being diagnosed at the right time. The lesson that I learnt from my illness was we parents, especially mothers, in the mad race of parenting ignore ourselves quite a bit. It is time we stopped doing that and took care of our health. I have learnt the lesson of my life the hard way and I don't want any other parent in this world to go through the same.

Epilogue

I have tried to make the book as inclusive as possible, which is why you will see issues of parents with infants, toddlers, pre-teenagers, teenagers and grown-ups being addressed. I have cited examples from my own experience along with inputs from psychologists and clinical psychiatrists, some of whom are also friends. The book talks at length about the things parents are confused about. Although I am not an expert, I have tried to balance my personal journey with the suggestions of experts. I have dedicated a chapter to parents who have special children and what it is like when your child's sexual orientation is not the same as the parents'. I could not have had a book for parents without sharing my fatal experience with sepsis and my struggle with a severe autoimmune disease, as I know that parents inevitably worry about who will take care of their children in their absence. I wrote about my struggle with sepsis and my journey to recovery in the last chapter of this book, originally published in *The Hindu*. I hope this book helps parents from all walks of life and also those who are planning to become parents!